Soccer Training

Soccer Training
Games, drills & fitness practices

Malcolm Cook

Forewords by Sir Bobby Robson, CBE,
Mark Hughes, MBE and Jeff Tipping

Eighth edition

A & C Black • London

Note

Whilst every effort has been made to ensure that the content of this book is as technically accurate and as sound as possible, neither the author nor the publishers can accept responsibility for any injury or loss sustained as a result of the use of this material.

Published by A&C Black Publishers Ltd
36 Soho Square, London W1D 3QY
www.acblack.com

Eighth edition 2010
Seventh edition 2003
Sixth edition 1999
Fifth edition 1997
Fourth edition 1994
Third edition 1992
Second edition 1988
First edition 1984

ISBN 978 1 4081 1480 3

A CIP catalogue record for this book is available from the British Library.

Acknowledgements
Cover photograph © PA Images
Inside photographs © Getty/PA Images
Illustrations by Mark Silver
This book is produced using paper that is made from wood grown in managed, sustainable forests. It is natural, renewable and recyclable. The logging and manufacturing processes conform to the environmental regulations of the country of origin.
Typeset in 11 on 13.5 Stempel Garamond by Saxon Graphics Ltd, Derby

Printed and bound in the UK by Martins the Printers

Contents

Christiano Ronaldo, the Real Madrid and Portugal player and World Player of the Year 2008, has practiced diligently over the last few years to scale enormous heights in performance and become one of the most feared attacking players in world football. When he was first signed by Manchester United he was dismissed by many critics as a 'one-trick pony' who could only dribble with the ball on his own. However, he practiced relentlessly with his coaches and became the complete and devastating player that we see today.

Acknowledgements

A special thank you to three coaches of the highest quality who I hold in high esteem: namely Sir Bobby Robson CBE, Mark Hughes MBE and Jeff Tipping, director of education and coaching at the NSCAA, for your excellent forewords.

Forewords

Having worked in the Football Industry field for over thirty five years, I have found that players, and teams, respond best to a programme which is simple, varied, progressive and maintains interest for all through its sound organisation.

Players want to see improvement in their game, whilst enjoying the work at the same time – and this is precisely what this book does, in a clear, instructive and logical fashion. The manual presents coaches, trainers and teachers with a wide range of ideas for improving and developing their players techniques and skills, and also gives them an insight into tactics and specific football fitness programmes.

Author Malcolm Cook, who has a vast experience in football coaching, has produced an excellent practical book that I am delighted to recommend to coaches, trainers and teachers at all levels of the game.

The late Sir Bobby Robson, CBE

The late Sir Bobby Robson, CBE
Fulham, Ipswich Town, England, PSV,
Barcelona, Porto and Newcastle United

Every coach, whether a beginner working with children, or an experienced professional club or national team coach, requires a pool of soccer knowledge, and a portfolio of technical practices and fitness training sessions in order to provide their players with a structured coaching and development programme.

Using simple language and clear diagrams, this excellent book provides these tools. The basic principles of coaching and training are explained clearly and simply in a format which can be used on a daily basis by the working coach.

Malcolm Cook is a professional coach with extensive experience of professional club coaching,

Mark Hughes, MBE

player development and coach education. I fully endorse his book, and consider it a welcome addition to the literature available on soccer coaching and fitness training.

Mark Hughes, MBE
Former Manager of Welsh National Team,
Blackburn Rovers and Manchester City

Malcolm Cook is a true Da Vinci Coach ... he has done it all and is still a master of the craft of coaching. The process of coaching is much more than rolling a ball out and blowing a whistle when something goes wrong – it is making a real contribution to the sport, leaving a legacy and helping to make boys and girls into good men and women. In my work as Director of Education for the National Soccer Coaches Association of America we are always on the lookout for quality books to recommend to our members. I thoroughly recommend *Soccer Training* and every book that Malcolm has written for coaches. The NSCAA is a world-class coaching organisation and I am pleased to recommend to our 31,000 members the work of Malcolm Cook, a truly unique individual."

Jeff Tipping

Jeff Tipping,
Director of Education and
Coaching Development,
NSCAA

Theo Walcott, the Arsenal and England forward, is beginning to realise the expectations placed upon him earlier in his career. He has, under the astute coaching of Arsene Wenger, added a more consistent end product to his dynamic dribbling skills. Continuous practice sessions have improved his crossing delivery of the ball and his ability to score more goals. This practice routine is a never-ending process for young players who want to fulfil their potential in the game.

Introduction

This book is designed to offer systematic coaching and training programmes for soccer based on sound learning principles. It contains fundamental games, drills and practices that can be organised with the minimum of equipment to develop technical skills, tactical understanding and fitness. All the activities are challenging and interesting, and coaches and players alike will be able to measure progress.

The book is divided into two parts. Part one contains drills and games which are set out to develop technical skills, goalkeeping and tactics of the game, and caters for all players. The activities begin from a basic level, gradually increasing in difficulty, thus extending the players in a systematic fashion. Part two provides information and guidance on the major fitness practices of aerobic fitness, anaerobic fitness, strength training, core stability, agility, and flexibility.

The emphasis throughout is on purposeful, enjoyable and progressive activities that add variety to the routine of regular soccer training which can be a drudge and also unprofitable if players are provided with the same activities at each practice session. This book will ensure that the soccer coach has a wide repertoire of games, drills and practices at his finger-tips to improve his players' technical skills, tactics and fitness. I have tried wherever possible to provide games or game-like activities, as I believe this is the best way to learn the sport.

Note: Throughout the book soccer players and coaches are referred to individually as 'he'. This should, of course, be taken to mean 'he or she' where appropriate.

Part 1: Coaching

Control and passing

Dribbling, screening and tackling

Crossing and heading

Shooting

Tactical games

Indoor games

Goalkeeping

Introduction

To obtain maximum benefit from a practice session the coach should pay attention to three organisational elements.

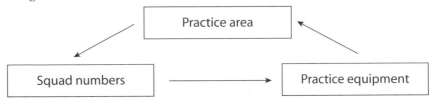

Practice area

Space must be utilised properly and practice areas designated for the squad if the game is to have full effect. Basically, the coach has two 'types' of practice area from which to choose.

(1) Grids These are a series of squares marked on the ground, measuring 10 × 10yds, and usually set out on surrounding grass areas to the playing pitch. The grids are flexible and can accommodate large numbers of players working together to improve their technical skills or tactical play by joining or splitting up the squares. For example, in the diagram below, area A measures 20 × 20yds, area B measures 30 × 20yds, area C measures 40 × 20yds, and the total working area measures 40 × 60yds.

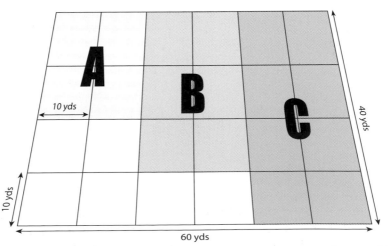

(2) Playing pitch It is often not possible, or even necessary, to have grids marked on the playing pitch, since its own markings with varying dimensions and shapes, can be utilised most effectively. In general, the game should take place in the *direction* and *area* where the players mainly operate in their respective functions during the actual game. However, this is not always possible due to the changing state of the playing pitch – particularly muddy goal mouths. Whatever the area selected, the coach must ensure that the dimensions are realistic for the number of players at his disposal, otherwise the game will lose much of its effectiveness. As a rule of thumb the following guide-lines apply: games to develop dribbling, screening and tackling should have 'tighter' areas; games for shooting should have a shorter and narrower pitch to encourage shots; crossing and heading practices require a shorter, but wider, area for crosses to be delivered well. Passing and control are best performed in a medium size area; long passing requires a longish and narrow area. As improvements are made, the general dimensions can be reduced so that the players learn to perform their technical skills and tactics in tighter circumstances – just like the 'real' game.

Coaching

The games and drills described in the following chapters can be used by the coach for his squad of between 12 and 22 players. The games, which are designed to develop individual technical skills and group or team tactical play, are used by top coaches from all over the world in various forms to improve their teams and players. Some of the games are 'old-time favourites', while others are more recent; however, they have all been tried and tested and can be recommended to the soccer coach for use with his squad during practice sessions. All are set out logically, showing the purpose, organisational requirements, procedure, scoring, development and coaching points. The advantages of these games are as follows:

Continuity
The games have little or no stoppages, and plenty of action with everyone involved in continuous play where they can learn skills or tactics in a realistic way.

Simplicity
The games are easy to organise, with simple procedures for scoring and setting up. The coach can leave players unsupervised to some extent, knowing that their interest will be maintained and that learning will still take place even though he may not always be directly present at the practice.

Coaching
The design of the games means that players get maximum repetition of certain technical skills and tactical play – cutting down the need for long verbal descriptions or demonstrations from the coach. The key coaching factors can be given by the coach beforehand, leaving the players with more practice time in which to perfect their performances.

Progression
The coach can make the games more or less difficult to suit the ability/range of the players in his squad by:

- **player numbers** – adding or subtracting players so that one group, having an added numerical advantage, 'outweighs' another, thus giving them success by either making their task easier or more difficult as they start to improve

- **practice area** – reducing or enlarging the practice area to put more or less pressure on technical skills or tactical play by giving players more or less space and time in which to perform

- **practice rules** – introducing new rules or 'conditions' for certain individuals, or all players involved in the game, to stress a particular technical skill or tactic. The condition can either make things a little easier or more difficult for the player. For example, some players could play 'free', with as many touches of the ball as required, while others would only play 'one-touch' as their condition.

As a rule, the coach should look to give players early success with new skills or tactics, and should then gradually progress by making success more difficult to attain by increasing pressure on the players' and squad's technical skills and tactics.

Competition

The games have a 'built in' competitive scoring element which can be used by the coach to improve the players' performances if he introduces group team competitions. Each player's performance within a given time limit is totalled up and added to the group team score for comparison. This will help to maintain the motivational level of the players and also to reproduce their technical skills and tactical play in the actual competitive game more effectively.

To get the best out of the games, the coach should consider the following:

Conditions

The 'conditions' to any game or rules, the 'punishments' for infringements, and the awards for goals, etc., must be communicated clearly to all players involved in the game so that there are no misunderstandings.

Supervision

When the coach is not available to supervise a game, try to delegate a player who is acting as ball retriever to be referee, with power to award free-kicks and deduct points, and generally see that the rules of the game are followed. A player with authority will be best able to handle the situation, e.g. the team captain or another senior player.

Patience

The players and the coach will need patience when learning to play a new game, since errors will be made until they become familiar with the rules and general demands of the game. The coach must see that the players do not give in too soon, and must show patience and perseverance at all times, especially with skills and tactics they find particularly difficult.

Finally, the coach should remember that these games are not an excuse for him to neglect his coaching duties; the value of the games is in their easy organisation and design, which will give him many opportunities to teach specific technical skills or tactical objectives in some depth.

Squad numbers

The coach will need to deal with varying numbers in his squad, depending on players' availability. The coach can add to, subtract from or generally manipulate his squad to emphasise attacking or defensive aspects of play. Players who are surplus to immediate requirements should still be actively involved in the game by acting as servers or retrievers of the ball. To provide better organisation and motivation for players, it is best to have several small group 'teams' within the squad, each with a definite role to fulfil for a set period of time before 'rotating' in order to change roles with another group team. In this way, the coach can keep all the players involved in a competitive game.

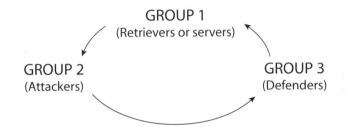

GROUP 1
(Retrievers or servers)

GROUP 2
(Attackers)

GROUP 3
(Defenders)

Practice equipment

Safe and easy, portable equipment is important for marking out the practice areas for the squad. Coloured traffic cones are lightweight and not only give good visual impact and clear identification of the games areas, but they can also be used quickly to alter the sizes of an area. Corner posts with sharp points can be driven through holes in the centre of the cones and into the ground to make a more stable goal. Where stated in a game, full sized goals, either portable or static, should be used with nets for realism. Where this is not possible due to cost etc., the goals, each 8yds wide, should be made up with posts and cones as described. Coloured training bibs or shirts will help with identification and make the game more enjoyable. The number of balls at a coach's disposal is important as some games can only be played with a certain number. The quality and weight of the balls are also important; if they are too heavy, too light or distorted in shape they can spoil the continuity of a game. For example, heavy balls may prove painful for players during heading games.

Control and passing

SHUTTLE DRILL
Purpose

To develop short/medium/long-range passing techniques and ground/aerial control.

Organisation

Players line up in two files facing each other, with the first player on one side with a ball at his feet. He proceeds to pass it directly across to the first player on the other side, following in the same direction to join the back of the line and await his next turn. The player receiving the ball controls it and passes it back across to the next player on the opposite side; he also follows the ball to join up at the rear of the line, and so the sequence continues. Players must not run directly in the same line as the pass, otherwise he will block the next pass; he should run wide outside the line of the ball.

To progress, condition play to 'two-touch' and then 'one-touch' soccer and record which group achieves the most accurate passes in a given time period. The area may be widened or lengthened; players can perform other techniques, such as instep pass, chipped pass, chest control or bended pass.

Key points

- ☑ technical – use various techniques to pass/control the ball
- ☑ maintain good rhythm – 'control–pass–move'
- ☑ relax – use sensitive 'touch' with the ball.

ONE-TWO PASSING DRILL
Purpose

To develop wall-passing techniques.

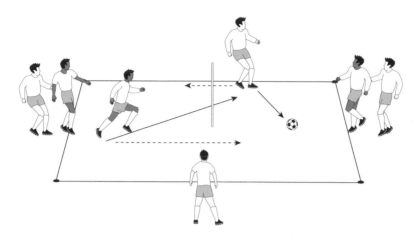

Organisation

Players arrange themselves in two files and stand opposite each other in an area approximately 30 × 20yds wide. A post is placed at the centre of the area. The leading player from one file plays a firm pass to the feet of the next player on the opposite side who comes at a wide angle to meet the ball. The latter then relays it first-time behind the post so that it coincides with the passer who should have run forwards to receive the ball and complete the one-two passing move. Both players carry on to their respective sides and the next two players from each file proceed to play a wall-pass from the opposite direction, and thus the sequence continues.

To progress, count the number of successful wall-passes in a given time period. Instead of a post, use an active player who must stay and defend the central zone while the players from both sides try to play wall-passes past him. The wall-pass, in this case, can be played to either side of the defender.

Key points

↘ first pass should be firm and accurate

↘ second pass should be soft

↘ both players to time their actions to keep possession.

TRIANGLE DRILL

Purpose

To develop basic reverse passing and controlling techniques.

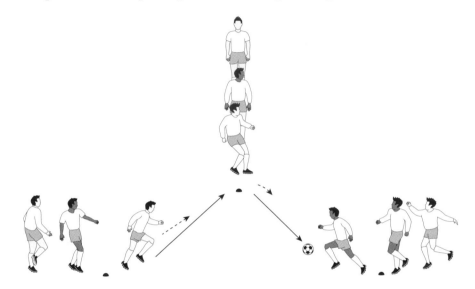

Organisation

Three files stand at cones; only one player has a ball at his feet. These cones are approximately 10–30yds away from each other in a wide-angled triangle. One player from each group stands at a cone with a ball at his feet. On the signal, the player with the ball passes it to either of the first players positioned at the other two cones, and follows the ball past the player who is receiving his pass. The player then goes to the end of that team's line to await his next turn. Each player must control the ball to face another line before passing and following it.

To progress, count the number of successful passes in a given time period. Condition play to one- or two-touch control and passing. Impose set techniques, such as chip pass, chest or outside of foot control or passing. Introduce another ball to increase pressure on the players; the two balls should be kept in motion.

Key points

   ↘ decide how you will control the ball, then relax
   ↘ pass the ball simply, quickly and accurately
   ↘ run at speed in a circular shape to the back of the file.

CIRCLE DRILL

Purpose

To develop general passing and controlling techniques, as well as awareness of where to pass the ball.

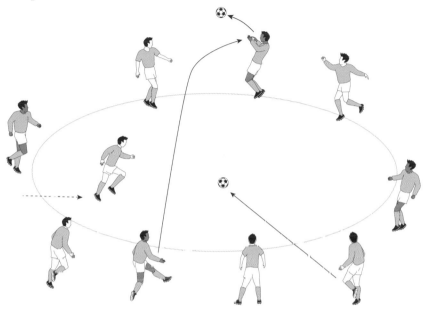

Organisation

A group of players stands around the centre circle. One player passes the ball across the circle to the feet of another and immediately follows his pass to change over with the player, who then controls and passes to another player in the circle. Players are not allowed to pass to those on their immediate right or left side. Any player who gives a poor pass, or collides with the ball as they are both travelling across the circle, must collect the ball before joining up with the drill again.

To progress, the coach can impose certain conditions, such as controlling the ball with the outside of the foot, looking for a bended pass, or only passing with the weaker foot. As players improve, the coach can introduce a second and then a third ball, which should be in motion at the same time. Players in this situation should call out an individual's name before passing the ball to him.

Key points

- keep looking around – be prepared
- control the ball by relaxing as you touch it
- make up your mind quickly – pass with accuracy.

THE SQUARE

Purpose

To practise general passing and controlling skills, as well as ball possession and tackling.

Organisation

In an area 40 × 40yds square, teams play 6 v 6 possession soccer. If a team executes a set number of consecutive passes without the opponents touching the ball, the latter are 'punished' by having to sprint through the 'gate' (made up with posts at one corner), around the square and back inside the gate again to rejoin the game. As soon as one team attains the agreed number of passes the other team is allowed 30 seconds in which to cover the 160yds. As soon as time is signalled, the team inside the square starts another passing sequence to try to achieve the required number of passes to send the opposing team around the square again. The penalised team must set off immediately after the agreed passes to get as many players back into the square as they can by the time 30 seconds have elapsed.

To progress, any player who 'gives' the ball away with an unforced error drops out of the game, leaving his team a player short; he can only come back when his team regains ball possession. Impose conditions, such as two-touch soccer, or the use of a no tackling rule – only interceptions allowed.

Key points

- quick – simple passing decisions
- move into spaces as soon as you pass the ball
- as defenders – press as a group.

PIG-IN-THE-MIDDLE GAME
Purpose

To develop passing and controlling skills, and ball possession.

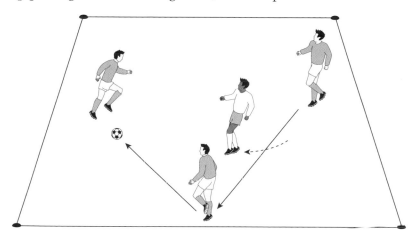

Organisation

In an area 10 × 20yds, four players play 3 v 1 soccer. The player acting as the defender should wear a brightly coloured shirt or bib for clear identification. The game starts with the three attackers playing two- or three-touch soccer, with the 'pig' trying to get the ball and knock it out of the square. Groups can play for set time limits agreed by the coach, such as 30–45 seconds, before changing over so that another player becomes the 'pig-in-the-middle' (e.g. the last player to give the ball away). The highest number of consecutive passes attained by a group of three makes them the winners.

To progress, the coach can impose conditions, such as one-touch play or passing with the weaker foot where possible. Groups can be increased to play 4 v 2 and 6 v 3 in a larger area.

Key points

- ➘ control ball quickly, accurately with 'touch'!
- ➘ time your passes at the correct moment
- ➘ move to the best position to help your team-mates.

SWITCH PLAY GAME

Purpose

To practise possession passing and switch passing.

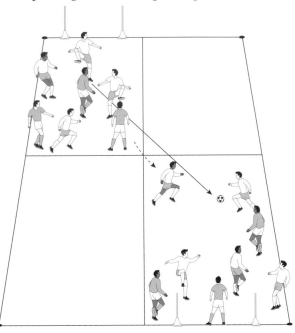

Organisation

Play is in an area approximately 40 × 40yds square, which is 'quartered', with small goals (without goalkeepers) diagonally opposite each other. Five players play three defenders in one quarter, while 4 v 3 players wait in the other quarter. The five players play possession soccer until they achieve a set number of consecutive passes, e.g. 3–6, whereupon one of them can play a switch pass to a team-mate in the other quarter zone. As soon as the pass is made, the *nearest* attacker sets off to join his team-mates and make it a 5 v 3 game where they try to score in the small goal. Whether they score or not, as soon as the attacking outcome is known, the five attackers start a passing build-up again and look to switch play back to the other quarter zone with a new player running to link up. Change players over.

To progress, the coach can impose conditions, such as one- or two-touch play.

Key points

- be patient when passing for possession
- try to disguise your 'switch pass'
- players should make good runs 'off the ball' to receive passes.

OVER-THE-GAP GAME

Purpose

To practise aerial and long passing, possession play and controlling skills.

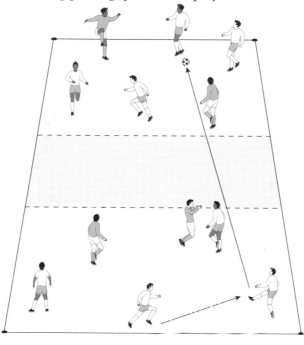

Organisation

An area 60 × 30yds is divided into thirds; four attackers versus two defenders play in each of the final zones. All groups must remain in their own respective zones. On the signal, one of the sets of four attackers plays two-touch soccer while looking for the opportunity to play the ball over the gap to one of the four players in the other end zone. The defending players must try to block or intercept the passes (at first they can be restricted).

To progress, condition play and only allow players to pass a long ball after a certain number of passes has been achieved. One or two extra defenders can be situated in the 'no-man's-land', thereby increasing the difficulty for the players in making the long ball pass.

Key points

- patient play to maintain ball possession
- quick, relaxed techniques to deliver the long passes
- good, sensitive 'touch' to control the ball.

GIVE-AND-GO GAME
Purpose

To develop quick one-two passing and controlling skills.

Organisation

Use an area approximately 25 × 15yds. Six players stand outside the rectangle and two inside it, one as a 'give-and-go' player with a ball and the other acting as a defender to intercept the ball. The attacker can screen the ball and pass it to any of the six players situated outside the rectangle, looking for a quick return pass to go past the defender. The six players can play the ball among each other but should take the chance to play it to the player inside the rectangle whenever possible. They are also limited to one- or two-touch soccer. The game is physically strenuous and for this reason the two players inside the area should be changed over at regular intervals.

To progress, count the number of successful 'give-and-go' passes in the allotted time period. The players can be limited to two, or even one-touch play. The player 'on the ball' should look to move up and down the rectangle.

Key points

- take ball towards the defender to commit him to challenge
- pass it quickly and firmly past him to outside player
- run past on the other side for the return pass.

SILENT SOCCER GAME
Purpose

To develop passing, support and possession play, awareness of team-mates and running off the ball.

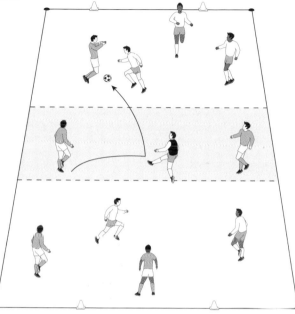

Organisation

In an arca approximately 60 × 40yds wide, two teams play 5 v 5 soccer with no goalkeepers and small goals. A line is marked 15–20yds from each goal: to score a goal the player must be inside this 'scoring zone'. This will encourage a passing build-up. A spare player who acts as as 'floater' must be a support player for whichever team has possession of the ball, and he does not need to defend. He should wear a different coloured shirt or bib from the rest to help identification. The teams play possession soccer and try to score in the small goal; if any player *calls* for the ball then a free-kick will be given against his team. This will encourage the player 'on-the-ball' to look around quickly before passing.

   To progress, the team scoring the most goals wins. Impose conditions, such as 'follow your pass', 'control and pass' or look for wall-passing opportunities.

Key points

   ↘   player on ball to get his head up to look for best passing option
   ↘   play mostly simple passes but look for defence splitting ones!
   ↘   keep looking for best position to support your team-mates.

KEEP-BALL GAME
Purpose

To practise basic possession play and penetration.

Organisation

Use an area approximately 25 × 15yds wide; six players are stationed around the outside of the rectangle with another two positioned inside. The six players who are not allowed inside the area interpass, while the two defenders who are not allowed outside the area try to intercept the ball. Whichever player has a pass intercepted should change places with one of the defenders. The coach must insist that the ball stays on the move all the time and never becomes stationary.

To progress, players can be awarded points for maintaining possession of the ball, and extra points if they manage to execute a pass which travels along the length of the rectangle and penetrates the two defenders. The coach can impose conditions, such as one-touch passing, passes below knee height, or control before passing.

Key points

- use varied passing techniques (eg. outside of foot, back-heel etc.)
- give yourself time by relaxing
- play quickly or slowly depending on the situation.

BREAK-OUT GAME

Purpose

To practise general ball possession and timing of passes, and runs off the ball.

Organisation

Use an area 50 × 20yds, which is divided up so that there is a middle 10 × 20yd zone. 13 players are arranged in the following way: five attackers play possession soccer against two attackers in the end zone. They must achieve a set number of consecutive passes *before* a pass can be played by one of them into the middle 'free zone' for another attacker to break out of his square, collect the ball and run with it to the other end square, linking up with four attackers to play 5 v 2 possession play. These five attackers play as before until they reach the set number of passes, when one player breaks out to link up with the other side again. The defenders are *not* allowed in the middle zone, nor are the attackers allowed to dribble the ball into it or stand waiting in the zone for the ball to arrive (offside rule can apply).

To progress, players can be conditioned to two-, or even one-touch play, or the pass played into the central zone must be a specific type, e.g. wall-pass or chipped pass. Extra players can be introduced, or the dimensions of the practice area reduced, to increase pressure on the group.

Key points

- quality passing with disguise, pace and accuracy
- timing of runs with through-passes
- movement of players to maintain ball possession.

BLOCKADE GAME

Purpose

To develop penetration play and patient possession soccer.

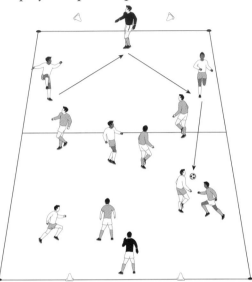

Organisation

In an area approx. 60 × 40yds, six players play six with goalkeepers in portable goals. The rule is this: if a team scores a goal it is *not* allowed to get another until the other team scores one. The players who have lost a goal push their goal off the field and play 'keep-ball' possession soccer for as long as they can before defending their goal when they eventually lose the ball. Their goalkeeper, who has no goal to defend, becomes an outfield player; the team with the goal to defend is not allowed to pass the ball back to the goalkeeper, since this encourages negative play. A free-kick is awarded for infringements of play. The nature of the game is such that one team is encouraged to attack 'all-out', while the other is encouraged to play 'tight' possession soccer.

To progress, the team which has no goal to attack (because it has already scored) may be given an added incentive by awarding points for high numbers of consecutive passes. Impose the condition of one- or two-touch play, on one or both teams.

Key points

  ↘ good support positions to get possession of the ball
  ↘ quick, simple and accurate passing
  ↘ counter-attacking-forward passing and running.

CONDITIONED PASSING GAME
Purpose

To develop general passing and controlling skills, and support play.

Organisation

The players play 6 v 6 soccer in a 60 × 40yd area. The coach can impose the following conditions to achieve the above aims. All passes must be played over a 10yd range; no supporting player must come nearer than this distance to the player on the ball, otherwise a free-kick will be awarded to the other team. The game helps to discourage bunching around the ball. If any pass is given in a backward direction, then the next one must be passed first time in a *forward* direction. This will encourage penetration. The player who last passed the ball must follow his pass and support the receiver. This prevents each player from standing and admiring his pass, and makes him give immediate support to his team-mates. Each player, or specific players nominated by the coach, is only allowed two touches of the ball every time he receives it. This encourages players to control and pass the ball at speed.

To progress, all violations of the rules should be 'punished' by the award of a free-kick against the offending team. The coach can award points for individuals or teams who are successful in the chosen conditioned play.

Key points

- keep your head up to see best passing options
- control the ball away from the challenging opponent
- good support positions for man on-the-ball.

CROSS PASSING DRILL

Purpose

To practise varied passing and controlling skills with little space or time available.

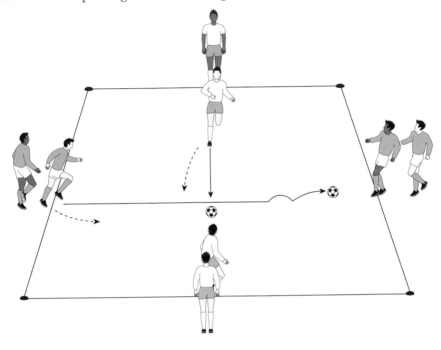

Organisation

Four files of players stand in a cross formation about 10–20yds apart with the first two players from adjacent files with a ball at their feet. One player passes the ball across to his counterpart opposite, quickly following it across to join the back of the line. The other player, as soon as he spots a gap, passes the ball to his respective side and likewise runs across to join the other group. Each player controls and passes the ball across to his opposite side, keeping two balls on the move at the same time, ensuring that he doesn't hit another player or the other ball as he does so.

To progress, condition play to two- or even one-touch of the ball as the players improve. Players must concentrate to ensure they do not hit the other ball with their pass.

Key points

- ➘ quick decisions – to control or pass?
- ➘ emphasise relaxation and fine-touch
- ➘ player receiving ball to move to the sides for the ball.

Dribbling, screening and tackling

DEFEND YOUR BALL GAME

Purpose

For attackers: to practise basic dribbling, screening and running with the ball.
For defenders: to practise basic tackling techniques.

Organisation

Each player dribbles his ball under control inside the 20 × 20yd area while trying to tag another player with his hand. Any player who is tagged or loses control of his ball so that it rolls out of the area must leave it before collecting his ball and re-joining the game. As players improve, instead of tagging each other, they can try to tackle and knock other players' balls out of the area, at the same time as controlling and defending their own balls.

To progress, extra points can be awarded for the successful execution of set techniques, e.g. sole of the foot dribble. Reduce the area or add more players to create congestion. The individual who has knocked the highest number of balls out of the square, or has the most points for losing control of the ball, wins the game.

Key points

- sensitive touch of the ball – keep ball near feet
- assertive use of the body to screen the ball
- careful tackling from behind opponents.

GET A BALL GAME
Purpose

To practise dribbling, screening and all-round tackling.

Organisation

The organisation layout is the same as for the previous game. The game starts with each player dribbling his ball inside the square; two other players wait outside without a ball. On the signal the two players enter the area and tackle any player to win a ball for themselves, which they then dribble and 'protect'. If any player is forced to play a ball outside the area, or he loses possession to a tackler, then he must challenge another player to try and get the ball.

To progress, reduce the size of the area or add more tacklers without balls to increase the degree of difficulty. The individual who has won the most tackles, or who has kept possession of his ball for the longest time, wins the game. Ensure that defenders tackle correctly from the back.

Key points

- dribble with the head up
- don't screen statically – keep on the move with the ball
- show patience when defending.

PRESSURE DRILL
Purpose

To practise timing tackles when fatigued, and basic dribbling skills.

Organisation

In an area 20 × 20yds, two small goals are situated on the corners of one end of the rectangle, which has been split into two halves. The squad is broken up into small groups, with one player acting as the defender; the rest line up facing him with a ball at their feet. On the signal each player, in turn, tries to dribble the ball past the defender to score in either of the small goals. The dribbler can only score from the coned zone, while the defender is allowed to tackle for the ball and knock it out of play from anywhere in the rectangle. As soon as this happens, or if a goal is scored, the next dribbler sets off to attack.

To progress, use different techniques, e.g. block tackle or change-of-pace dribble. Each defender can be given a set time period, e.g. 1 minute, and points awarded for the least or most goals scored in that time.

Key points

- take the ball towards the defender to unbalance him
- the defender should turn 'side-on' to the attacker
- defender to 'back-track' whilst staying balanced.

SLALOM DRILL
Purpose

To practise techniques for speed running with the ball.

Organisation

Slalom runs are marked with poles or cones, in an area approximately 25 × 10yds. The squad is arranged in small groups behind the slalom, with the leading player having the ball. On the signal, the player proceeds to run and dribble the ball through the slalom, finishing with a straight speed run and placing his foot on the ball so that it is stationary for the next player. This continues until each member of the group has had a go. Any player who misses a pole or comes out of the zone must return to the last pole before re-starting his run.

To progress, perform varying techniques or 'tricks' on the ball with both feet, increase the number of runs, increase the difficulty of the slalom by adding more posts, or give points to whichever group completes a set number of runs in the fastest time.

Key points

  ↘ keep the ball well in front of your feet
  ↘ 'sweep' the ball with your foot as you run
  ↘ keep your head up.

1 V 1 GAME

Purpose

For attackers: to practise dribbling, screening and turning with the ball to beat a player. *For defenders*: to practise jockeying for the ball and various tackling techniques.

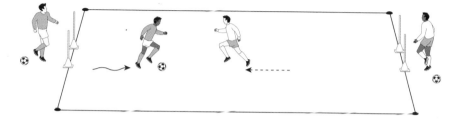

Organisation

Two teams play in an area of 20 × 15yds, with a small goal at both ends. Players in the two teams are numbered. The first from each play 1 v 1: the player with the ball tries to dribble past his opponent and score by pushing the ball through the goal. If the player scores he then immediately defends his goal against the next opponent while the beaten defender retreats behind his own goal to await his turn to defend or attack again. If the defender wins the ball he can score in the opponent's goal – the more successful he is at dribbling, the longer he will be in action. If the ball goes out of bounds, it should be returned by other players so that play is continuous.

To progress, the individual who scores the most goals wins the game. Extra points are awarded for a particular technique which is performed successfully, e.g. front foot tackle, or beating a player by playing the ball past him on one side and collecting it on the other.

Key points

- encourage 'tricks' to beat opponents
- effective use of the body when dummying and screening
- defenders/attackers to keep skills going when tired.

CONDITIONED DRIBBLE GAME
Purpose

For attackers: to practise dribbling, screening and turning with the ball to beat a player. *For defenders*: to practise intercepting, jockeying and tackling for the ball.

Organisation

An area approximately 40 × 30yds wide is marked out and split into two halves. The game is 5 v 5, with each team having three defenders and two attackers who are restricted to their own half of the area. The game begins with one of the back players dribbling and later passing the ball with the other back players. They have to get the ball up to one of their two colleagues in the opposite half who, in turn, look for opportunities to screen and dribble the ball past opponents until one of them carries the ball under control over the end line to score a point. The attackers cannot pass the ball *over* the end line; also, defenders must make their tackles *before* the attacker reaches the end line. The sets of players should be changed around so that all experience dribbling and tackling practice.

To progress, limit the number of passes that attackers can make to encourage dribbling and tackling. Give attackers or defenders extra points for successful displays of set techniques, e.g. tackling with the weaker foot only, or turning with the ball to beat a player. The team with more 'goals', or fewer against them, wins the game.

Key points

- good touch of the ball – use both feet to dribble
- encourage attackers to go at defenders with the ball
- defenders to 'jockey' and show patience.

Aaron Lennon, the Tottenham and England winger, is a young player with high potential who is looking to build the consistency required to make the position his own with club and country. He has explosive pace, the ability to take the ball around defenders and can on occasion cause havoc to defenders. Like all promising young footballers, he will need to put in years of varied practice to learn new skills and tactics to continually refine his existing technique.

TAKE-OVER DRILL

Purpose

To practise take-overs while running with the ball.

Organisation

In an area approximately 25 × 10yds, two files of players face each other; one of the leading players has the ball. On the coach's signal the player runs with the ball under control towards one side of the next player on the opposite line. As he approaches with the ball, the receiving player performs a take-over and carries the ball on to the next player on the other side, who then takes it from him. The drill continues in this way until all the players have had a turn.

To progress, on a signal, the take-over player pretends to take the ball but actually performs a 'dummy' manoeuvre, leaving the dribbling player to carry on with the ball. Give points to the group that completes a set number of runs with the ball in the fastest time. Remember to start slowly until your timing improves – be safe!

Key points

- use the same foot when running with the ball
- disguise the take-over
- accelerate away with the ball.

Crossing and heading

KEEP-UP DRILL
Purpose

To practise controlled heading techniques.

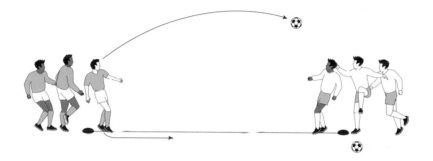

Organisation

Players line up in two files facing each other, about 2 or 3yds apart. The first player tosses the ball up in the air and heads it to the first player on the *opposite* side, while moving in the direction of the ball to join the end of the far line and await his turn to head the ball again. The next player heads the ball to the player opposite him and moves to the back of that file, and so the sequence continues. The players keep the ball in the air with their heads only.

To progress, count the total number of consecutive headers. The coach can ask players to perform two successive headers before playing the ball to the next player. A static player can stand between the files so that all headers have to be played over him.

Key points

- make contact on forehead
- head under the centre line of the ball for height
- put the correct pace on the ball.

NON-STOP ATTACK
Purpose

To practise crossing and heading techniques.

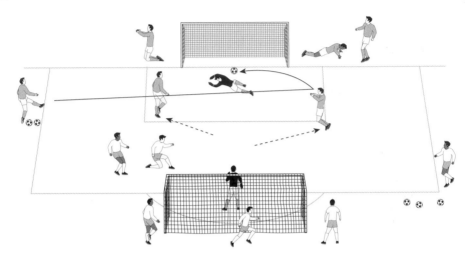

Organisation

The squad is divided into two teams, each with six players and one goalkeeper, in an area 20 × 40yds wide. Three players act as retrievers, two as attackers looking for headers, and the last one from the team crosses the ball. The game starts with one of the wingers crossing the ball for the two attackers to come to the near and far goal post areas to head for goal directly, or to set up one-touch shooting chances. As soon as the header, or shot, is taken the winger on the other side of the area crosses for his two attackers who must start from, and return to, their cone each time. The players change over after a set time period.

To progress, count the total number of headed goals per individual and group. Allow the goalkeepers to come out for crosses, and add a defender to challenge for the ball.

Key points

- ↘ good contact under and through the ball as you cross it
- ↘ correct pace on ball – near, mid-goal or far post
- ↘ watch the flight of the ball to time your header.

THROW- OR VOLLEY-HEAD-CATCH
Purpose

To practise general heading skills.

Organisation

Two teams play in an area 40 × 30yds, with full-size goals at each corner. The game starts with a player throwing the ball into the air for a team-mate to head so that another team-mate can catch it and restart the throw-head-catch sequence again. The player about to throw the ball must not be obstructed by opponents; however, once the ball is in the air they can jump to challenge for the ball. A free throw is awarded to a team when one of their opponents fails to head a thrown ball. If goalkeepers are used, they should be limited to their own goal lines.

To progress, the coach can introduce a volley-head-catch sequence where the player volleys the ball from his hands instead of throwing it. Allow players to double-head the ball when convenient, rather than catching it. Count the total number of headed goals.

Key points

- ensure two handed serves, high and accurate
- safety at all times – arms down, time your jump to avoid collisions
- use your body to spring high and attack the ball.

CLEAR THE DECKS GAME

Purpose

To develop crossing techniques and defensive heading skills.

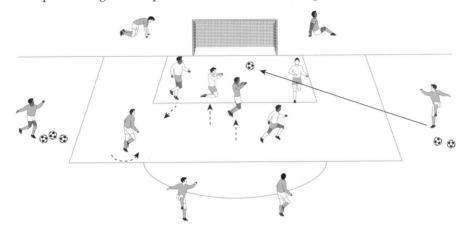

Organisation

The squad splits into three groups of players. One group acts as ball retrievers, another as defenders and the last group has two players as attackers and two as crossers. The wingers, who have a good supply of balls, each cross a ball in turn into the penalty area, but **not** into the goal area which is 'no-man's-land'. The four defenders, lacking a goalkeeper, try to head the ball out of the marked out area while the two attackers attempt to score with headers or challenge for the ball. If the defenders fail to use sufficient power to 'clear the decks' so that the ball does not land past the penalty area line, then the two attackers who are positioned outside the penalty area can combine with the attackers and try to score while the four defenders come out quickly to block the shot. If the ball is cleared by a header which lands past the line, then the ball is returned to the wingers who cross alternately.

To progress, count the total number of headed clearances and goals scored against the defenders. Extend the danger zone so that headers need to be more powerful, and add another attacker to the penalty box.

Key points

- cross with a relaxed action and follow-through
- ensure defender's footwork is dynamic as they prepare to face the cross
- attack the ball.

END-TO-END HEADING GAME
Purpose

To develop crossing techniques and attacking/defending heading skills.

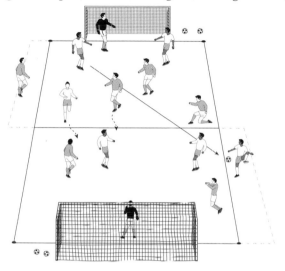

Organisation

The squad divides into two groups, each with a goalkeeper who is always in action. The game is played in an area approximately 40 × 50yds wide, which has goals at each end plus a channel for a winger from each team to play inside. The teams play two-touch soccer and try to get the ball quickly to their own winger, who is restricted to the attacking half of the field and cannot be tackled in his channel. The winger crosses the ball for attackers to attempt to score with headers while being challenged by defenders. At the conclusion of every attack the goalkeeper rolls the ball to one of his team-mates who has just been defending and his team tries to get the ball to their winger so that they can attack the other goal. Corners can be played, as can throw-ins and free-kicks. The goalkeeper may be restricted, initially, to his goal line.

To progress, count the total number of successful headed clearances and goals scored. Allow the winger to move out of his channel and another attacker to move into it to cross the ball. Allow the goalkeeper to take crosses.

Key points

- ensure the crosser focusses on the ball as he strikes it
- select the best crossing option for each situation
- attackers and defenders should get to the ball first.

BOXED-IN GAME
Purpose

To develop crossing and general heading skills.

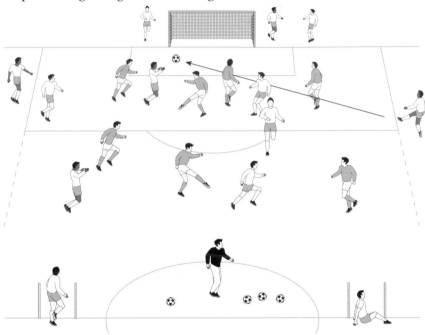

Organisation

Four defenders play three attackers: they are all restricted to the penalty box, and there is no goalkeeper. Outside the box five attackers play against three defenders with the restriction that these eight players are not allowed in the box. The five attackers play possession soccer and try to set up crosses from varied positions into the box for their three team-mates to score with headers, while defenders try to clear the ball through one of the two small goals at the end of the field. The number of players can be altered depending on whether the coach wishes to emphasise attacking or defensive heading, or put more pressure on the crossers.

To progress, count the number of headed goals or successful clearances. The coach can condition the game so that wingers must play first-time crosses.

Key points

   ↘ the rhythm and slight turn of the hip as the crosser strikes the ball

   ↘ keep your feet moving to enable fast jumping

   ↘ practice timing jumps early or late as you head the ball.

WAVES OF ATTACK
Purpose

To practise varied crossing and heading situations in attack.

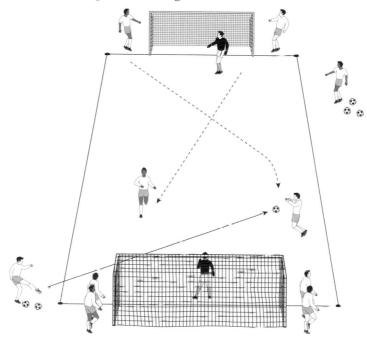

Organisation

Eight players form up in pairs at the sides of two portable goals about 20yds apart, each defended by a goalkeeper. Two players stand on opposite flanks with a good supply of balls. The first pair of attackers attacks the other goal by a cross-over run to look for the cross to the near or far post region, where they try to score with a headed goal. As soon as the attack ends, another pair of attackers immediately comes from the other end to look for a cross, and thus the practice flows from end to end.

To progress, ask the servers to cross a specific type of service for a set period, e.g. far post, diving header at near post, etc. Add a defender to give him defensive practice or to make it more realistic and difficult for the attackers.

Key points

- ↘ relaxed body action – sweep leg under/through the ball
- ↘ timing of runs – near post early, far post later
- ↘ decision to head for goal or set-up team-mate.

Shooting

TWO-TOUCH SHOOTING GAME
Purpose

To develop basic shooting techniques.

Organisation

The squad is split into groups of three, with one player acting as goalkeeper. The drill takes place in an area 40 × 15yds wide. Posts are placed in the ground 8yds apart, half-way up the length of the area. Each player is allowed two touches of the ball before he shoots at goal; if the goalkeeper saves the ball, or if it travels past the goal, it is collected by the other player who then shoots as the goalkeeper turns to face the shot. The players change over after a set time period and scores are recorded.

To progress, the players can practise varying techniques, such as volleys or swerved shots. Another player may be introduced to act as a defender and put in challenges to add more realism to the game. Make sure players hit the ball on the move, which is more realistic.

Key points

- approach the ball from the side smoothly
- place your non-kicking foot comfortably to the side of the ball
- swing your foot through the ball.

LAY-OFF DRILL
Purpose

To develop varied shooting techniques while on the run.

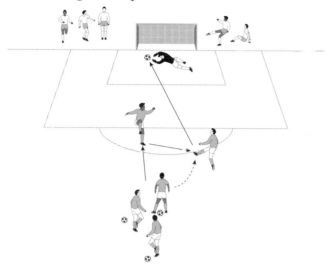

Organisation

The squad is organised into two small groups, one of which acts as ball retrievers, while the other group practises. The drill takes place in the penalty box area where a goalkeeper defends the goal. One player stands in the 'D'; the other players, each with a ball, stand in a file facing him, approximately 20yds away. The first player in the line passes the ball to the feet of the player in the 'D', who proceeds to 'lay' it off for the former to shoot at goal. The 'lay-off' player then goes to either cone A or cone B to collect a ball from the retrievers before returning down the side to join the file and await his turn. The player who has just shot at goal becomes the next 'lay-off' player and faces the second oncoming player. In this way, each player shoots, and acts as the wall-player.

To progress, each group is timed for a set period and the scores tallied up. The coach can impose certain conditions, such as shooting with the weaker foot, or volleys from the 'lay-off' player flicking the ball up for another player to hit at goal, or long-range shots. Record the number of goals scored in a given time period.

Key points

- ensure players 'lay' ball off with correct pace accurately
- watch oncoming player hesitate slightly before running to shoot
- keep toes stretched out as contact with the ball is made.

CHANGE-OVER GAME
Purpose

To create and take shooting opportunities.

Organisation

Two teams (A and B) use an area 60 × 30yds. A goal, 8yds wide, is marked with posts and defended by a goalkeeper. Play is 5 (A) v 4 (B) in one half of the area – A's fifth player is positioned in the other half. B's five attackers make use of the extra player and combine to shoot at goal. When the ball enters the other half B's four defenders join up with their colleague and become the attackers, while four players from team B move into that half to defend. This leaves one player behind and creates the 5 v 4 situation once again. As soon as the ball enters the other half, the nearest defenders must come out quickly to block the shot.

To progress, encourage shooting by making the players play one- or two-touch soccer. Shots which hit the target after a first-time strike gain extra points.

Key points

 ↘ encourage players to shoot at every opportunity
 ↘ look to follow all shots in
 ↘ stay as relaxed as possible when striking the ball.

SHOOTING ON THE TURN GAME
Purpose

To develop players' ability to shoot in turning situations.

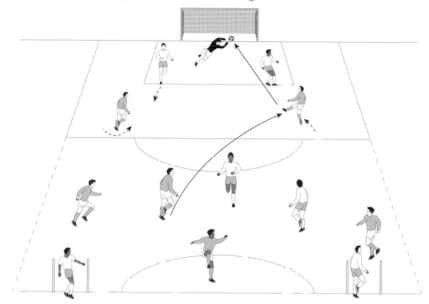

Organisation

The game takes place from the width of the penalty area up to the half-way line where two small goals are placed on the sides of the area. The squad is split up into three teams with one goalkeeper; one team acts as ball retrievers. The attacking team has two players who are restricted to the penalty box – the other attackers are not allowed inside. The two defenders stand inside the goal area while the others play outside the penalty box. The out-field players attempt to play the ball to one of their colleagues in the box who, in turn, tries to turn and shoot or lay the ball off for his team-mate to shoot first time. One of the defenders may leave the penalty area to make a challenge when the ball enters the box, while the other blocks the goal. If the defenders win the ball they attempt to play it through one of the small goals.

To progress, the coach can impose the condition that the two attackers are only allowed one pass inside the penalty box.

Key points

- attackers to get into the 'half turned' position before the ball arrives
- keep 'switched-on' to shooting opportunities
- swivel and shoot in one motion.

COLLECT AND SHOOT GAME

Purpose

To develop quick breaks and create early shooting situations.

Organisation

The squad is divided up into three small groups: one of the groups retrieves the balls, while the other two play attack versus defence in an area stretching from the goal line to the half-way line. A supply of balls is left in the centre circle. The game starts with the goalkeeper and all the other players stationed inside the penalty area. The coach calls a player's name and he runs to collect a ball and dribble it forwards, while the other players combine with him to try to get a shot at goal. If they win the ball, the defenders play it to one of the retrievers on the half-way line.

To progress, the coach can put increased demands on certain players by regularly nominating them to collect the ball. Each group can be given a set time limit and goals are recorded. The coach can impose conditions, such as two-touch soccer, forward passes only, or first-time shots only.

Key points

- first attacker to run at speed towards the goal with the ball
- look for a direct shot, wall-passes or to dribble the ball
- all players to look for shots as the first option or decision.

ON-TARGET GAME

Purpose

To develop controlled shooting skills.

Organisation

The squad is divided into three groups, that retrieve the ball or defend/attack in the game. The game is played in the same area as for 'Collect and shoot', with two small goals on the half-way line. The coach has a few balls in the centre circle; when he passes a ball to a player this signals that the **team with the ball must attack** and attempt a shot at goal, while the **other team must defend** and try eventually to play the ball through one of the small goals. If the defenders manage to do this, then they receive the next service from the coach and attack the goal, while the other team now defends. However, should the attacking team get a shot on target they receive the **next** service, or if they manage to score they receive the next **two** services.

To progress, the coach can 'punish' teams that shoot inaccurately when not under pressure, or that fail to accept shooting chances, by giving the next service to the other team. The coach can impose one- or two-touch play to quicken shooting.

Key points

- ↘ take every opportunity to shoot
- ↘ follow all shots in − look for rebounds
- ↘ attempt shots from all distances, angles and situations.

PRESSURE SHOOTING DRILL

Purpose

To develop quick-reaction shooting skills.

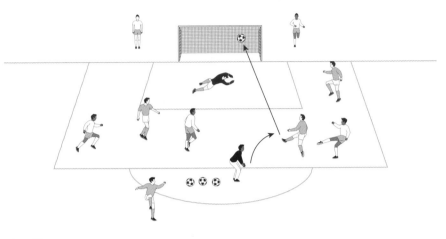

Organisation

The squad is divided into three groups and a goalkeeper. The coach stands outside the penalty box and half-circle and serves balls into the area for players to shoot quickly at goal. The service is indiscriminate and whichever player gets to the ball first shoots, or passes to a team-mate who must shoot **first time**. The service must be continuous and each team is timed for a set duration before changing over its role. The coach can serve a variety of techniques, such as the volley. The team which does not have ball possession must challenge immediately to prevent shots and force shooting errors.

To progress, the coach records the teams' scores and gives added 'bonus' points for players who perform difficult techniques, such as overhead shots at goal.

Key points

➘ keep 'switched-on' to react quickly

➘ be prepared to shoot whilst off-balanced

➘ good decisions – to shoot or pass quickly.

LONG-RANGE GAME

Purpose

To develop long-range shooting skills.

Organisation

In an area approximately 50 × 40yds, set up two portable goals on the end lines and single posts on the half-way line. The squad is divided into three groups and two goalkeepers: one group retrieves while the other two practise in the area. The teams play 3 v 1 in each half of the area; the attackers set up shooting chances for each other, while the one defender challenges for the ball. The three players can pass the ball to their isolated team-mate in the other half but can only receive return passes in their own half. The advanced player can look for deflections or 'knockdowns' from the longer shots to follow in and score. The game fluctuates from end to end, with the goalkeeper serving the ball for a team-mate to attack the other end as soon as a shot is hit at goal.

To progress, conditions such as one- or two-touch play can be introduced. Other attacking and defending players can be added. The coach can allow any of the three players to pass the ball to a team-mate in the other half and break forwards to shoot at goal. Do not allow long passing sequences – limit them to ensure more shots at goal.

Key points

- smooth approach to the ball
- decide on target area
- strike through the ball with full power.

SURPRISE SHOOTING GAME
Purpose

To escape tight marking and to take unexpected shooting changes.

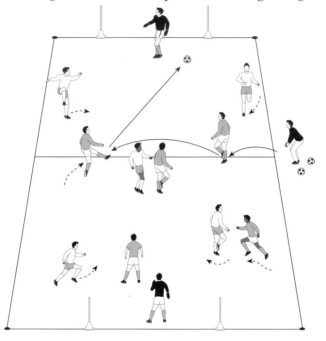

Organisation

The squad is split into three groups, with two goalkeepers in action throughout the game – two portable goals are placed on the end lines. The coach receives balls from the servers to keep the game continuous. He serves the ball to a player whose team attacks and tries to score, while the other team defends, although if they win the ball they can attack. As soon as an attack is completed, the coach should serve the ball to the other team, thus ensuring that play is end-to-end.

To progress, the coach should occasionally play the ball to players in situations where they will have to react quickly. The coach can impose conditions, such as only allowing one or two players from each team to score. The scores should, as always, be recorded.

Key points

- be mentally and physically prepared
- react quickly to scoring opportunities
- decide when to shoot, pass or dribble the ball.

Tactical games

CONDITIONED OFF-THE-BALL GAME
Purpose

To develop off-the-ball attacking play.

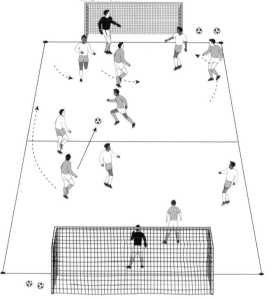

Organisation

In an area approximately 60 × 40yds, the squad plays 6 v 6 soccer, with goalkeepers and portable goals. The coach imposes certain conditions on the players for a short duration, which if violated are punished with freekicks. Some conditions include:

- each player must overlap the colleague to whom he passes the ball
- specific players must get into and attack the space behind the rear defenders
- players look to make blindside runs behind defenders and out of their vision – or in front of them to pull them out of position.

To progress, extra points can be awarded to players who perform off-the-ball movements successfully.

Key points

- deciding what type of run to make
- deciding where to run
- deciding when to run.

CLOSING-DOWN GAME
Purpose

To develop defensive closing-down play.

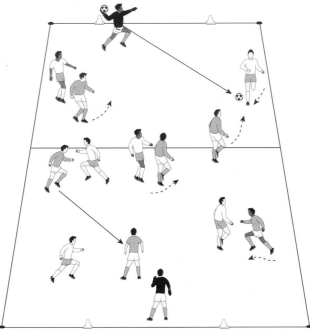

Organisation

On an area 60 × 40yds the squad plays 7 v 7 soccer, with goalkeepers and portable goals. The coach imposes the condition that the *nearest* defender to the player with the ball each time shouts 'One!' to indicate clearly to all that it is his responsibility to close the attacker down, which he attempts as soon as he has shouted. If he fails to do this he is punished with a free-kick against his team. As the defensive organisation improves the next player in a covering position behind 'One' shouts 'Two!' to indicate that his role is to cover.

To progress, the coach can teach players to close down the correct distance and angle. Players who close down effectively and prevent the ball going forwards, or actually win the ball, can be awarded extra points by the coach.

Key points

- make decision to press the ball quickly
- shout the number clearly to let other team-mates know what you are doing
- come in fast to the opponent but under control.

Only the 'best of the best' footballers manage to win the World Player of the Year award and Lionel Messi, the Barcelona and Argentina 'playmaker', accomplished this in 2009. Small, dynamic and elusive to challenging opponents, Messi's extraordinary talent is accentuated by many years of dedicated play and practice. However, like all top players, he does not settle for this, but continues to work hard on the training field to develop his game to its limits.

MAN-MARKING GAME

Purpose

To learn how to mark closely and how to escape this marking; also to practise the role of the 'sweeper'.

Organisation

The teams play in an area approximately 60 × 40yds, with the condition that each player in each team is responsible for marking and tackling his own particular opponent. If any player marks or tackles somebody other than the player he is delegated to watch, then a free-kick will be awarded against him. Each team has a 'free-man' or 'sweeper' who is restricted to playing in his own half of the field and to two-touch soccer. He can also cover his team-mates and intercept or tackle in his own half any attackers who have broken free from their markers.

To progress, restrict the sweeper to one-touch play only. Allow the sweeper to 'break' over the half-way line and into the opponents' half: the man-markers can leave their own opponents to challenge him if they feel it necessary.

Key points

- mark 'shoulder-to-shoulder' when the ball is near
- stand where you can see the ball and the man you are marking at all times
- attackers to dodge in all directions to escape marking.

FOUR-GOAL GAME
Purpose

To develop passing and switching play in attack, and cover and balance in defence.

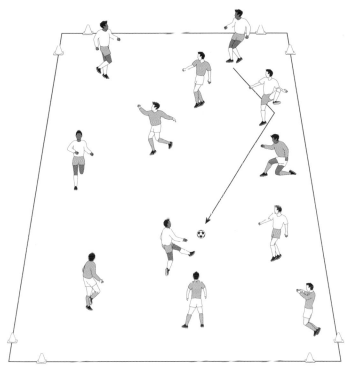

Organisation

An area approximately 60 × 60yds square is used; four small goals are placed at each corner. Goalkeepers do not play; each team defends two goals at one end and attacks the other two at the far end. The players play possession soccer and attempt to 'pull' the bulk of the defenders over to defend one goal before switching the ball suddenly towards the less well-guarded goal, and trying to score there.

To progress, play one- or two-touch soccer. The coach can award extra points for goals which come directly from the team switching play.

Key points

↘ maintain good support positions 'off-the-ball'

↘ play passes accurately and quickly to feet

↘ look to change the direction of passes when appropriate.

KEEP THE PRISONER
Purpose

To develop defensive closing-down, cover and balance.

Organisation

A large circle approximately 50yds in diameter is marked around the centre circle with cones. One attacker is restricted to the area inside the centre circle, while his colleagues play 6 v 3 soccer in the outer area. The six attackers play possession soccer and try to finish with a pass to the colleague inside the circle; the three defenders work to prevent them doing this. The defenders can run across and through the inner circle; however, they are now allowed to stop and intercept passes inside this area. Players change over after a set time period.

To progress, initially, do not allow attackers to play the ball above knee-height, but as defenders improve withdraw this restriction. Add more or fewer players, depending on the success of the game. Time each trio of defenders for a given period: the group which concedes the least number of passes wins the game.

Key points

> ↘ press as a group
> ↘ first defender to get in 'tight' should work to prevent forward pass
> ↘ cover players to position at sides.

BUILD-UP GAME
Purpose

To develop controlled passing play from the back region of the team up to the front.

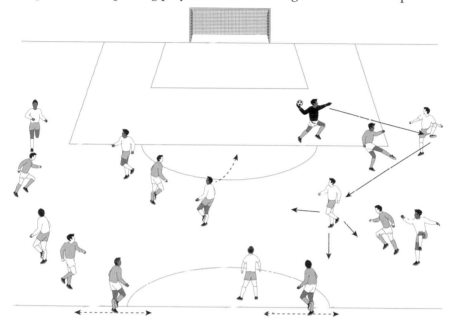

Organisation

On half a full-size pitch, the squad is split up into defenders and attackers in an 8 v 5 situation, with a goalkeeper, and two players restricted to being able to move only *along* the half-way line. The game starts with the goalkeeper rolling the ball out to a player; the team then interpasses until one of them carries the ball at his feet *unopposed* over the half-way line. The players on the half-way line can shuttle across the line to challenge any players approaching with the ball.

Passes cannot be played *over* the half-way line for players to run on to: the attacker must dribble the ball over to score a point. If an attack breaks down the ball must go back to the goalkeeper and the patient passing build-up must start again.

To progress, condition play to one- or two-touch passing; and add another defender to make passing more difficult.

Key points

- players to spread out quickly wide and long
- pass ball simply, quickly, and to feet
- when it is 'on' – run the ball over the halfway line at speed.

ALL-UP AND ALL-BACK GAME

Purpose

To develop compact team play.

Organisation

In an area approximately 60 × 40yds, with portable goals on the end lines and a half-way line marked on the area, two teams play soccer with the following condition of play: for a goal to count, the entire team must be over the half-way line and into the opponents' half of the area when the final header or shot is struck.

To progress, a team can be awarded *two* goals if they score with their players over the half-way line *and* if they catch 'stragglers' from the opposition who have not managed to get back into their defensive half of the area when the goal is scored. Attackers who cannot get back are punished by a free-kick being given to the opposition from the point at which they were caught.

Key points

- ↘ controlled passing and movement
- ↘ team to move up/back in time with the ball speed
- ↘ all players to keep 'switched-on' and concentrated.

RE-START GAME

Purpose

To develop the squad's re-start organisational play.

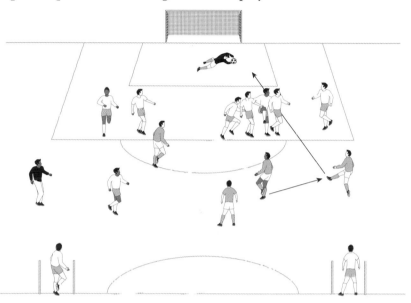

Organisation

The squad plays attack versus defence in one half of the field, with the distribution of players depending on whether the coach is working on attacking or defensive play. Two small goals are placed to the sides of the half-way line; two players, who have a supply of balls, act as servers and retrievers behind these goals. The attackers receive the ball from one of the servers and proceed to attack the goal; the defenders try to protect their goal and win the ball, playing it as quickly as possible through either of the two smaller goals. The coach blows his whistle to indicate real or imaginary offences which result in free-kicks, corner kicks or throw-ins for the attacking team. This gives both attackers and defenders practice in dealing with re-start situations.

To progress, the coach can award extra points for 'special' ploys which are demonstrated successfully.

Key points

- ↘ look to take quick restarts where possible
- ↘ all players to concentrate at all times
- ↘ practice difficult situations repetitively.

Indoor games

BENCH PASSING CIRCUIT
Purpose

To practise short passing and control techniques.

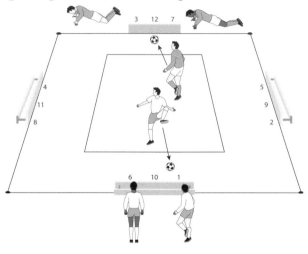

Organisation

Four benches are laid on the floor and numbered, as indicated, from 1 to 12. A small inner square, or rectangle, is marked on the floor, approximately 15yds from the benches. The group is organised into two small teams and one player from each team stands in the inner square or rectangle with a ball at his feet. On the signal a player moves forward and passes the ball against the bench from 1 to 2, 2 to 3, 3 to 4, and so on until he reaches 12. Each player must hit the numbered area, making sure that he passes the ball from *inside* the inner area every time and always controls the ball *outside* it before bringing the ball back to face the next number.

To progress, the team which completes the circuit in the fastest time wins. The players can be conditioned to use set techniques, such as weaker foot to control or pass, outside of foot only, sole of foot control, etc. Two players, one from each team, can compete against each other: one moves from 1 to 12 while the other moves in the opposite direction and passes from 12 to 1. Whichever player finishes first wins.

Key points

- pass at correct pace and angle
- control ball in direction of next bench
- move with ball close to feet.

SOCCER SQUASH

Purpose

To develop driving, volleying and control techniques.

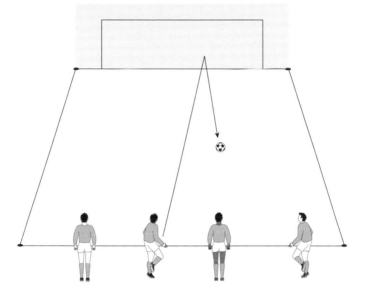

Organisation

A long goal, about 10 × 2yds high, is marked on a wall and a 'shooting line' marked on the floor approximately 15–20yds away from the wall. The group is organised into two small teams numbered from 1 onwards. Each player from each team drives the ball into goal in rotation. After a player has struck the ball at the goal, the next player, behind the line, controls the rebound off the wall before he in turn drives the ball at the wall. Any player who misses the target, hits the ball with insufficient power, or fails to control the ball properly either loses a point for his team or drops out of the game; play re-starts with the next player.

To progress, the coach can impose conditions, such as use of weaker foot only, flick ball up into the air before volleying at goal, control ball while in the air, etc. The coach can impose a time limit during which groups have to attain as many drive passes as they can. Different weight of ball can affect the height that they bounce and what techniques you want to practice.

Key points

- control the ball to set yourself up for volley
- make contact to spin/swerve the ball
- kick at good angles.

BENCH SOCCER
Purpose

To develop control, and short volleying techniques.

Organisation

Double benches, or a low rope or net, are used to section the court into equal halves. The players are split into teams and the game is played with a lightweight ball. The game starts with one player, who is positioned at the back of the court, tossing the ball up in front of himself and gently lobbing it with his foot over the benches and into the opponents' side of the court. The ball is only allowed to bounce once on the floor before being 'juggled' in the air with head, foot or body: it must be returned within a set number of touches into the opponents' side again. (Players are not allowed to volley in a downward direction.) Whichever team allows the ball to touch the floor more than once, or fails to return it over the bench and into the opponents' area, loses a point.

To progress, the first team to reach a set number of points wins the game. The coach can impose the condition that only one particular player from each team can return the ball, or the ball can only be returned with the weaker foot.

Key points

- relax when controlling the ball
- use all parts of the body to control/volley
- look to play the 'killer' volley to win the points.

CRAB SOCCER
Purpose

To develop strength, agility, control and volleying techniques.

Organisation

A small group from the squad is split into two teams that play in an area with benches, acting as goals, at each end. The players move around backwards, sideways or forwards in 'crab' fashion, keeping hands and at least one foot in contact with the floor to interpass, head, dribble and shoot to score by hitting the bench. The goalkeeper is allowed to sit or kneel on the mat and a penalty kick will be awarded if he gets up from the stated position. The other players are likewise punished if they get up from the floor, handle the ball or seek to gain an unfair advantage.

To progress, the team scoring the most goals wins the game. The coach can give extra points for goals scored by volleying the ball, thereby encouraging specific skills.

Key points

- players to ensure they spread out – no bunching
- good use of the body for volleys
- try 'new' techniques (e.g. overhead shot).

HEAD TENNIS

Purpose

To develop controlled heading.

Organisation

A net or rope approximately 5ft high is placed half-way across a 30 × 30yd court, and the game is played with a lightweight ball. The group is split into two teams that are stationed either side of the net. One player at the back of the court starts the game by tossing the ball into the air and heading it over the net into the other half of the court. The ball is only allowed one bounce on the floor; players must juggle the ball into the air with their feet for three successive headers from three different players before returning it over the net. A team loses a point if the ball bounces twice on their side, fails to go over the net and into the opponents' court, or is not headed by three players in succession. Teams scoring a point retain the service.

To progress, the team to score more points wins.

Key points

- good 'touch' of the ball
- contact under ball – keep it high
- set-up team-mates for 'killer' headers.

HIT-AND-RUN
Purpose

To develop control and drive passing techniques.

Organisation

Two players, wearing distinctive coloured bibs or shorts to make them easily identifiable, act as 'shooters' and interpass to try to shoot and hit the other players **below their knees with the ball**. The latter aim to dodge and evade the ball; they can use their hands to protect themselves if shots come at their face – **for safety purposes it is advisable that a lightweight ball is used**. Any player hit with the ball either loses a point or drops out of the game. The 'shooters' are given a time period in which to hit as many players and score as many points as they can.

To progress, make it more difficult for the 'shooters' by imposing a one- or two-touch condition, or allowing them to shoot with their weaker foot.

Key points

- awareness – keep looking around
- control ball quickly
- make contact higher up the ball to keep it low.

CHANGE SOCCER

Purpose

To develop general passing, control and awareness of the ball.

Organisation

Benches or small goals are placed at either end of the indoor area and the squad is split up into four smaller teams, with coloured shirts or bibs for identification. The teams sit in the corners and each is given a number from 1–4. When the coach calls out two numbers the relevant teams play soccer for a set period, and only retire to their own corners when other numbers are called. As soon as they hear their numbers, teams immediately defend the *nearer* goal and try to score at the other end. The coach, if he wishes, can keep both goalkeepers in action all the time.

To progress, teams can be handicapped by having to play with a player short, or they may be conditioned to one- or two-touch play. The team to score the most goals or win the most games wins the competition. Ensure the teams change over quickly.

Key points

- good control, passing and ball possession
- encourage screening and dribbling
- know when to play fast and slow.

CHAIN RUN

Purpose

To develop dribbling techniques and agility.

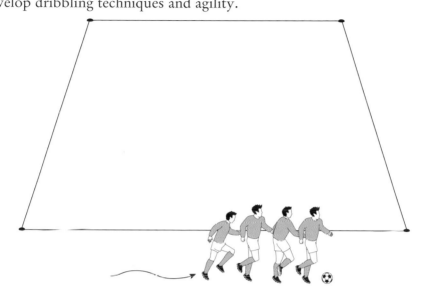

Organisation

An area approximately 20 × 20yds square is marked out, with posts positioned around the edges of the square. The squad is broken up into small groups; group players form a chain by holding the backs of each other's shirts. The leading player dribbles the ball around the circuit while the rest, keeping linked-up, move behind him. When the run is completed, the dribbler halts the ball and moves to link up at the rear of the 'chain'. The front player then dribbles the ball and the pattern continues until the entire group completes the run. If a team loses control of the ball, the players must retrieve it, maintaining the chain formation, and re-start the run where they lost control; similarly, if the chain 'breaks', players must return to their original positions.

   To progress, the coach can create competitions which keep to a set time schedule, increase the number of runs, or increase the difficulty of the circuit.

Key points

- watch that shirts are not held too tightly
- leading player must show good control of the ball
- other players to move at the team's speed.

TUNNEL BALL RELAY
Purpose

To develop short passing, running with the ball and agility work.

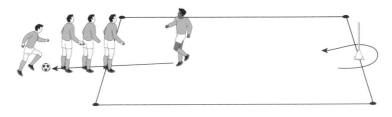

Organisation

The squad splits up into small groups of players that compete against each other in an area 20 × 10yds, with a marker post at each end. Players line up in a file behind a post with their legs opened wide to form a tunnel. On the signal, the first player in the team turns to face the rest of his players and push-passes the ball through the tunnel. The end player in the file then controls it before dribbling it around the post at the other end of the area, returning to the front of the file and passing it through the tunnel for the next player. This continues until the last member of the team has finished, or the team has completed a set number of runs.

To progress, the winner is the fastest team or the team which completes the most runs in a given time period. The coach can impose conditions, such as passing and running with the ball, using only the weaker foot, etc.

Key points

- keep ball well in front of yourself as you run
- steady yourself before passing the ball
- all players to stay close and keep their legs wide apart.

STEAL-A-BALL
Purpose

To develop dribbling techniques and awareness of the ball.

Organisation

An area 20 × 20yds square, with cones at each corner, is marked out. Four players are positioned at each cone and 16 balls are bunched together in the centre of the square. On the signal, the players run to the centre, dribble a ball back to their corner and place it by the cone. The first player to have *four* balls at his corner wins the game. Players cannot tackle each other but they are allowed to 'steal' balls from other players' corners when they are out of their areas.

To progress, prevent the game from becoming too lengthy by counting the number of balls at each player's cone after a given period of time: the player with the highest total wins the game.

Key points

- awareness – keep looking around
- keep ball close to your feet as you run with it
- decide quickly where to go for a ball.

Goalkeeping

SHUTTLE GOALKEEPING DRILL

Purpose

To practise various handling techniques.

Organisation

Players line up in files facing each other approximately 20yds apart, with a goalkeeper in each file. Cones are placed on the end lines to act as goals. While the rest of the players pass and follow the ball to the back of the line, the goalkeepers field the ball with their hands before rolling it to the feet of the next player from the opposite side and then following across. In this way the goalkeeper can join in a normal drill activity and practise his own specific techniques, while the other players practise their own particular skills.

To progress, the coach can ask players to try to push the ball past the goalkeeper to score in the goals. The goalkeeper attempts to dive and save the ball each time. The coach can direct players to give specific practice to the goalkeepers, e.g. play the ball high in the air for the goalkeeper to catch, drive the ball hard at his chest, or attempt to dribble the ball around the goalkeeper. Remember, the practice is designed for the goalkeeper, so be sure to give success each time and ensure safety always.

Key points

- ensure that body is side-on and low along the ground
- hands/arms parallel in front of body
- good hand shape to gather the ball.

SHOT STOPPING AND DISTRIBUTION GAME
Purpose

To develop positional sense and to practise handling and ball distribution.

Organisation

In an area approximately 30 × 20yds wide, two portable goals are placed on the end lines, with both goalkeepers facing each other and having a good supply of balls placed at the back of each goal. The first goalkeeper starts by rolling the ball along the ground to try to score in the other goal, while the opposite goalkeeper positions himself to save the ball. The ball should be played backwards and forwards as quickly as possible so that the pressure on both goalkeepers is continuous. As the practice develops the goalkeepers can use overarm throws or volley/half-volley kicks to try to score.

To progress, record which goalkeeper scores more goals in a given period. The goals can be moved nearer to each other or further apart to make saving in the former or distribution in the latter more difficult. A player can be placed within 10yds of each goal; he is allowed to score from any mishandling by the goalkeeper.

Key points

- ensure accurate throwing and kicking
- good positioning, angling and footwork
- try to catch the ball where possible.

CROSS BALL GAME
Purpose

To give the goalkeepers practice in dealing with crosses from the flanks.

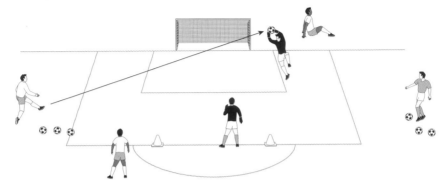

Organisation

A makeshift goal is set up directly opposite the permanent field goal about 20yds away. The two goalkeepers defend the goals, two wingers cover the flanks and one or two retrievers stand behind the goals. The wingers, who have a supply of balls, cross them into the 6-yd box in turn for the goalkeepers to catch or punch away to safety. If a goalkeeper catches the ball he immediately throws it to the winger on the opposite side, who then crosses it to his goalkeeper, thus maintaining continuity. After a time the same or other wingers should cross the ball from different flanks to give the goalkeepers practice in taking crosses from both flanks.

To progress, the coach can direct the servers to play specific types of cross to give the goalkeepers more difficult shots to deal with, e.g. leg in swinging crosses, near or far post balls or occasional driven shots. The coach can add a defender and one attacker to pose extra problems before adding more to the practice.

Key points

- good positioning at far post area
- face crosser and centre your body
- time the run and jump to catch/punch the ball.

TRIANGLE DRILL
Purpose

To develop agility, positional sense and shot stopping.

Organisation

A three-goal triangle of normal full-size goal dimensions is set up on a good diving area. Three cones are positioned about 15–20yds away facing the centre of the goals. One player stands at each cone, with at least two balls, while three retrievers stand around the area to get the balls back quickly to those at the cones. The drill starts with each player firing a shot at goal in strict rotation; the goalkeeper moves quickly from goal to goal to re-position himself for each shot. The coach should signal to players when they should shoot so that the goalkeeper is kept working hard to save shots. A reasonable time period for the goalkeeper is about 30–60 seconds, which the coach should monitor since the work is very strenuous.

To progress, create a competition among the goalkeepers to see who can lose the least number of goals in given time periods. Some of the players shooting the ball can be asked to play a certain type of shot, to give the goalkeeper practice in that situation. The coach can also increase the tempo of the practice thus putting him under greater pressure.

Key points

- good positioning off the goal-line
- ensure good body balance and footwork
- move quickly into the line of shot.

PRESSURE DRILL

Purpose

To develop quick reaction, positional sense and to practise handling and agility.

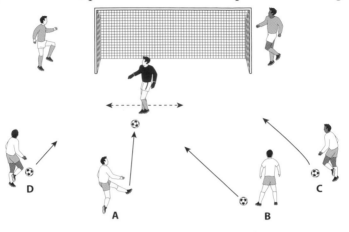

Organisation

A goalkeeper stands in goal, made up with posts, and faces varied serves from A, B, C and D in quick succession, for a set time period, as follows:

- ◣ A: stands approximately 10yds away, kicks a hard ball directly to the goalkeeper at chest level

- ◣ B: stands approximately 15yds away at an angle and drives a hard low shot for the near or far post region

- ◣ C: stands about 40yds away in a flank position and crosses a high ball in front of the goal

- ◣ D: who is positioned near the goal line and approximately 15yds away from the goal, hits the ball across the face of the goal.

The goalkeeper defends each service: if he saves the ball by catching it he returns it to the server, if not the three retrievers get the ball and keep the practice continuous.

To progress, count the number of successful saves made by each goalkeeper during a given time period. Quicken up the service, creating more pressure for the goalkeeper. Add an attacker who 'listens' near goal, and tries to score from anything that the goalkeeper fails to save.

Key points

- ◣ ensure good body shape and positioning
- ◣ solid footwork
- ◣ quick decisions/reactions to various shots.

TURNABOUT GAME

Purpose

To develop positional sense and to practise shot stopping.

Organisation

In an area approximately 30 × 20yds, two portable goals, defended by goalkeepers, are placed on the end lines. Each goalkeeper has two attackers and one defender stationed near his goal. The game starts with a goalkeeper rolling the ball quickly to one of the unmarked players, who is allowed two touches to either shoot at goal or pass for his colleague to shoot. As soon as the shot is hit the advance player nearer goal looks for a 'knock-down' from the goalkeeper and tries to score. As soon as the shot is dealt with, the goalkeeper then quickly rolls this ball out to set play going in the other direction, thereby maintaining the game's continuity. Use a few retrievers.

To progress, consider which goalkeeper loses fewer goals in a given time period. Add more players, thus creating more congestion for the goalkeepers.

Key points

- ensure good position, body shape and angle to shot
- footwork – skip along ground
- good 'touch' handling and catching of the ball.

HIT THE TARGET GAME

Purpose

To practise good all-round distribution of the ball.

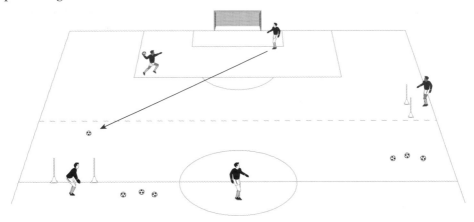

Organisation

Target areas are marked on realistic parts of the field; the goalkeepers, who should have a good supply of balls, in turn distribute the balls and try to hit the target areas where retrievers are positioned. The coach can award scores according to the degree of difficulty in hitting the different target areas, and the goalkeepers can perform under and overarm throws, goalkicks, and volleys and half-volleys from the hands.

   To progress, introduce an opponent to stand immediately in front of the goalkeeper to see that he complies with the four-step rule before distributing the ball. Players can be introduced to stand in front of the target areas and try to intercept throw-outs and kicks from the goalkeeper. Record which goalkeeper scores the most successful throws or kicks in a given time period.

Key points

- ensure smooth transfer of the ball between hands
- turn the body sideways on to the target
- full follow-through of the throwing arm.

WALL REBOUND GAME
Purpose

To develop agility, handling and quick reaction.

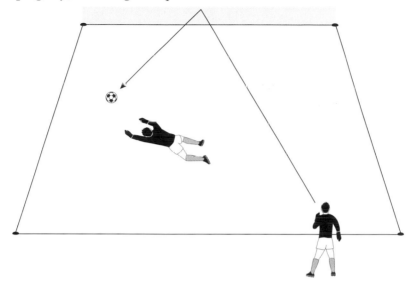

Organisation

The goalkeepers face a wall; lines are marked on the ground at various distances agreed by them. Generally, the nearer the wall the goalkeepers are, the more quick reflexes will be needed and shot stopping practised; if they use the lines which are further from goal, then they are more likely to work on distribution. The goalkeepers throw or kick the ball at the various targets marked on the wall, scoring points if they hit them. Later, one of the goalkeepers stands a few yards away from, and facing, the wall while the other goalkeeper, who is positioned behind him, throws or kicks the ball so that it rebounds from the wall. The goalkeeper nearer the wall is not allowed to watch the service, but dives to save the ball as it rebounds.

To progress, quicken the speed of the service, add another server so that the ball is served alternately from both sides, and determine which goalkeeper makes the most saves in a set time period.

Key points

- ensure good body shape
- footwork – keep feet moving
- push off ground powerfully.

DIVING SEQUENCE DRILL
Purpose

To develop good diving technique.

Organisation

A portable goal is set up in a soft diving area; the goalkeeper positions himself in the centre, a few yards in advance of his goal line, with the coach facing him several yards away. The coach serves him a set number of balls (6–12) or, better still, goalkeepers work in pairs and one defends while the other serves (they should change over after a set period). The server should deliver a certain type of ball in a set routine as follows:

- (1) a slow rolling ball
- (2) a bouncing or medium-height ball
- (3) a slow highball.

The goalkeeper should be stretched gradually by serving the ball further away each time (remember to serve the ball to *both* sides of the goalkeeper). He should also be made to use a set sequence of defence techniques, which progressively gets more difficult, e.g. laying on his side; squatting down on his heels; sitting to face the ball; diving over a ball or crouching player; on one/both knees; assuming a basic crouching position.

To progress, stage a competition between the goalkeepers, with a set number of serves each or a set time limit.

Key points

- ensure good body shape
- ensure good footwork
- use sensitive hands to catch or parry the ball.

DEFLECTION DRILL
Purpose

To practise diving full length to deflect goal-bound shots around the posts.

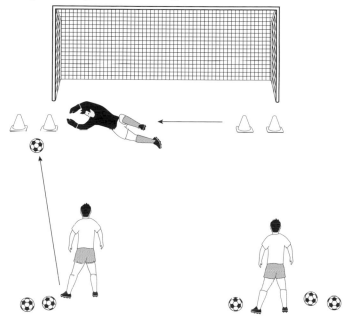

Organisation

Two small goals about 1yd wide are set up with poles or markers about 10yds apart. Two players with a supply of three balls each stand directly in front of the targets about 10yds away. The goalkeeper stands in the centre between the goals. The first server strikes the ball at a medium pace, trying to play it through the target as the goalkeeper moves across quickly in an effort to tip it with an outstretched hand around the post. As soon as he does this, the other server passes the ball into the other goal for the goalkeeper to recover and try to deflect the ball. He should have six continuous services to deal with. The servers need to time and judge their passes so that the goalkeeper can save the shot with difficulty.

To progress, move the goals further apart so that the goalkeeper needs to cover more ground to make his saves and vary the service to make things more realistic.

Key points

- fast, light footwork to move laterally
- body should be side-on to the shot
- stretch out long for shots.

Part 2: Games and practices for fitness

Soccer fitness components

The warm-up

The cool-down

Games for fitness

Summary

Introduction

This chapter aims to follow the general trend of the book in providing games or game-like activities, which can be used by the coach to develop physical fitness for football. Most of the games or activities can be further adapted to enhance particular elements of fitness, which may be specifically required by the players or team. It is not vital that you use these games for your whole fitness programme, as this is not realistic and, at times, other methods may be more suitable. However, by using games as part of your total fitness programme you will gain the following benefits:

- Specificity By replicating the type of movements, actions and running that is used to play the game, players are more likely to be able to perform better because everything they do in training is directly related to the game.
- Progression The games are designed so that they can be gradually intensified in terms of physical effort and difficulty. Fitness can be developed from a solid foundation up to an ever-increasing load throughout the playing season.
- Overload The training load should increase in a measured, progressive and systematic way so that players are prepared to deal with the considerable physical match demands. The principle of careful overload can be applied to all the games by the coach to achieve the desired training effect.
- Motivation All too often players complain that the training is boring. By introducing games or game-like activities with a competitive element in the correct way, the coach can sustain the hard work that players need to get fit for the game, albeit in a much more acceptable way. Players will find the games activities more realistic, enjoyable and purposeful and it will help them to get through the tougher training schedules that bit easier.

Soccer fitness components

Endurance

This is the ability to be able to perform for long periods of time in the game when fatigued and short of oxygen. The footballer needs to develop three kinds of endurance to allow him to express his skills, retain his mental concentration and perform well:

1. Aerobic The player has to endure continuous running during the game, which is of the cruising or jogging variety, but not flat out. He will usually have oxygen available.

2. Anaerobic The game makes many demands on players – they will have to make many fast bursts of speed with little opportunity to recover aerobically before having to go again.

3. Muscular Soccer also makes big demands on players' muscles during the game. The legs in particular have to be able to withstand much intensive work and must not fatigue prematurely.

All three types of endurance must be developed in any individual who is serious about becoming a good player.

Speed

There is no doubt about it – footballers in the modern game need to be quick! The ability to get off the mark and arrive at the ball first is essential for all players. Speed is a combination of mental reaction and fast physical movement – one always goes with the other. To become faster a player needs to practice and must learn how to react instantly, moving the body through explosive arm, body and leg actions in the most economical and fastest way.

Power

To apply your skills effectively a player needs power. He should firstly build a solid foundation of general overall body strength, before starting to convert this into the more specific power required to play the game well. He has to be able to transport his bodyweight all over the field whilst having the ability to be explode powerfully at any given moment in order to jump to head the ball, to tackle strongly for the ball or to kick the ball with real power at goal. Activities that allow players to move their own bodyweight powerfully at first before progressing to exercises using smaller weights, elastic-type bands and body harnesses will help to develop this quality.

Flexagility

This is a combination of flexibility, which is the ability to be able to achieve efficient stretching of the muscles, with agility, which is the ability to move and transport your body with speed and economy. Players need to be able to change direction and speed quickly before producing a dynamic skill. By improving this component, the player will benefit by preventing injuries and will gain quicker specific soccer movement and coordination for his skills. Flexagility can be improved by using dynamic stretching activities and game-type movements performed at speed.

The warm-up

Each training session should always be preceded by a warm-up, which uses progressive jogging, running and ball work. When the body's main muscle groups are suitably warmed-up it is time for them to be systematically stretched in preparation for the more intensive physical work to follow in the main part of the session. There are conflicting ideas over the merits of *dynamic* stretching (stretches whilst on the move) and *static* stretching (stretches whilst holding a stationary position). The majority of coaches would recommend that dynamic stretching is best done at the warm-up stage, to prepare players for the more strenuous work to come, whilst static stretching is best for the cool-down phase, to help players recover from the intensity of the session. Both types need to be conducted and carried out primarily with safety in mind, as they will not only help players to perform or recover better but will also assist them in preventing possible injuries. The coach must also be aware that the brain needs 'warming-up' in terms of getting the players mentally ready and 'cooling down' to bring them back to a more relaxed state.

The cool-down

It is equally important that players are assisted to allow their minds and bodies to recover from the hard physical work undertaken during the training session. There will be other training sessions or competitive matches to follow, so it is necessary to educate players to ensure they treat the cool-down just as seriously as they do the warm-up. Alongside the walking, jogging, light running, exercises and stretching work used, several types of games can be introduced that will be effective. Games of a light-hearted nature could be used to brighten those players whose moods may be 'down' after a defeat, and they are equally useful if the facilities available are poor and limited.

Games for fitness

"The Liverpool Box"

Whilst coach at Liverpool FC, I picked up this progressive running exercise routine, with and without the ball, which enables the group to work together in a gradually intensive way, building up endurance fitness.

1 AROUND THE BOX

Purpose

To develop aerobic endurance.

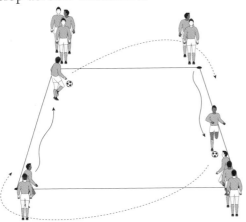

Organisation

Two files of players split up and face each other across a box approximately 30 x 30 yards. The first player in each file has a ball at his feet and they both dribble it across to the other side before leaving it for the next approaching player. They then run all the way around the box and back to the end of the line from which they started. Each player in turn repeats the circuit, making sure they always take the 'long way' round.

Progressions

To increase the work, the coach can ask players to move more quickly, increase the size of the box so that they need to run further or increase the amount of time that they have to complete each session.

DIAGONAL RUN

Purpose

To develop speed-endurance and agility.

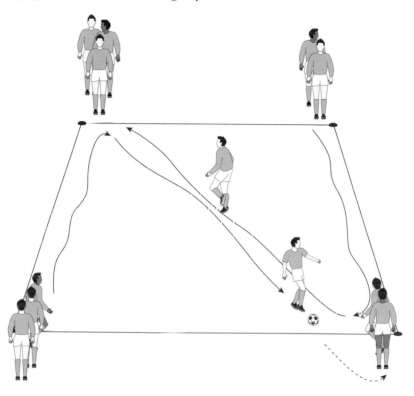

Organisation

Set up as 'Around the box' (page 94). Each player dribbles the ball forward to leave it, once again, with the approaching player opposite. This time however they turn quickly without the ball to change direction and sprint to the back of the other file to wait their turn to repeat the same movement on the other side. Therefore, after each dribble, the players turn and sprint diagonally to the other file. **Safety-check: Be aware of players running across the centre and colliding.**

Progressions

See the progressions for 'Around the box' (page 94).

TRIANGLE RUN

Purpose

To develop speed and 'flexagility'.

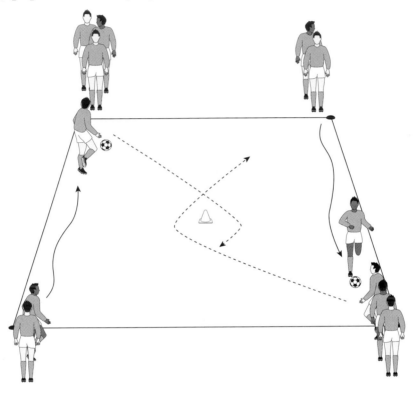

Organisation

The same set-up as before but this time each player dribbles the ball to the other side and then turns quickly without the ball to sprint and touch the cone positioned at the centre of the box. The player changes direction once again to return to the back of the file from where he started. **Safety-check:** The coach must ensure that players are made aware of the dangers of colliding as they run across each other during some of the exercises.

Progressions

See the progressions for 'Around the box' (page 94).

PASS AND RUN

Purpose

To develop aerobic, anaerobic and muscular endurance.

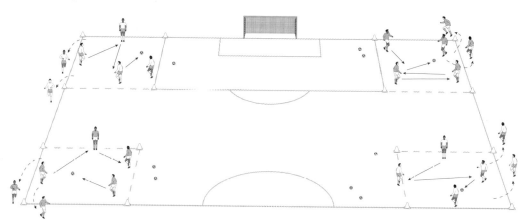

Organisation

On half a playing field, four 15 x 15 yard boxes are marked, with a few footballs lying handy on the ground near by. Eight players are paired up (e.g. 1 and 2, 3 and 4 etc.) and each group starts inter-passing inside their box. The coach signals/whistles and the first pair (e.g. 1 and 2) from each group proceed to leave their area and run together all the way around the half-field without the ball until they arrive once more back in their box. As they are running, the other six players in each box pass the ball around non-stop. As soon as the first pair return, the next pair (e.g. 3 and 4) break away to repeat the process as the rest of the group continue passing the ball inside their box.

Progressions

The coach can make the exercise more difficult by reducing the number of players in each group so that they have less recovery time, or he can use 'conditions' such as two-touch football or 'pass and move', which increases the running load. Alternatively, he can make it more competitive by awarding points to the first pair of players who get back to their box first.

PARLAUF RUN

Purpose

To develop aerobic and anaerobic endurance.

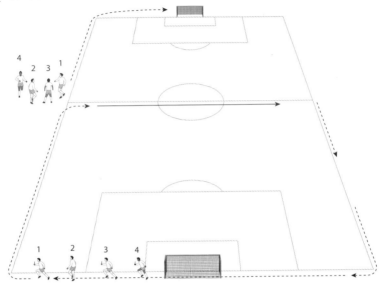

Organisation

On a full-size football field, the corners are 'rounded off' by markers to allow players to run more easily, safely and quickly on the bends. A group of players are paired up, one at each end of the halfway line, with either a baton or a ball at their feet. The first group with the batons race around the field with batons in hand before passing them to their partners on the halfway line at the other side of the field. Their partners then carry on running with the batons around the field, as the first group recovers by dribbling the ball across the halfway line so that they arrive in time to take the baton from their partner. They then continue running around the field as their partners slowly dribble the ball across the halfway line to meet up with them once again.

Progressions

A full-size field may be too big an area to start with, so it could be reduced to a half-field area. The coach can set a time period to see which pair completes the most laps of the circuit in the time given or just set them a number of laps to complete. This can be made competitive when the players are ready to cope with the increased physical demands.

UP AND DOWN THE CLOCK

Purpose

To develop aerobic and speed-endurance.

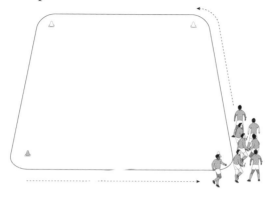

Organisation

Set up a box measuring approximately 30 x 30 yards with 'rounded corners'. Two groups of players stand at station one facing in opposite directions. The coach signals for the start and both groups run 'up the clock' as they move in different directions. Both groups should complete the following sequence:

1. Jog all the way around
2. Sprint one side, then jog three sides
3. Sprint two sides, then jog two sides
4. Sprint three sides, then jog one side
5. Sprint around all four sides.

The groups then run 'down the clock' in the following way:

1. Jog all the way around
2. Sprint around all four sides
3. Sprint three sides, then jog one side
4. Sprint two sides, then jog two sides
5. Sprint one side, then jog three sides.

Progressions

To increase the effort, the coach can intensify the distance by making the box larger or by making it more competitive between the groups.

CONTINUOUS SPRINT RELAY

Purpose

To develop speed-endurance.

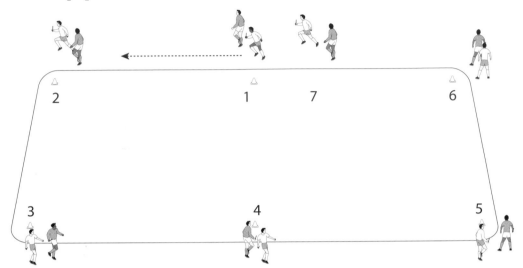

Organisation

On half a football field with 'rounded corners', a number of cone markers are placed at equal distances around the area. Two or more teams of seven players stand at each of the cones. The first player of each team has a baton. When the coach signals they proceed to race to the next station and pass the baton on to their next team member so that it moves quickly and continuously around the field. Always ensure that each team has an **extra man** at the first station to maintain continuity.

Progressions

The first team to arrive back at its original position wins and is awarded maximum points! The coach can increase or decrease the distances or the number of players or teams. Try to ensure that the teams have a relatively equal balance of fast players.

FITNESS CIRCUIT

Purpose

To develop power and muscular endurance.

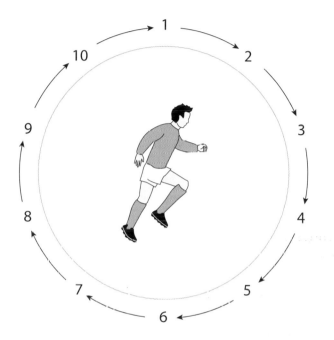

Organisation

A set number of exercise stations are placed around an area in circular fashion and a group of players move around them in sequence, working for a set period at each one before moving on to the next, until the whole circuit is completed. The exercises are arranged in the order of arms-body-legs to allow each muscle group to recover from the hard work before moving on to the next exercise. Here are the exercises and how they should be performed:

Station 1: Squat thrust

The player starts in the frontal press-up position with legs outstretched and body supported by his hands. He should drive his legs forward into the crouch position before returning both feet back to their original position. Players should work in a rhythmical fashion and count one each time their knees make contact with the inside of their elbows.

Develops: Arm, shoulder, stomach, back and leg muscles.

Station 2: Sit up

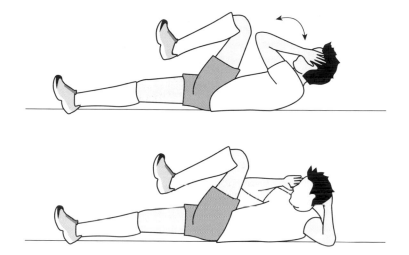

The player starts by lying on his back with knees bent and hands at the side of his head. He then raises his body upwards and brings his right elbow across to touch his left knee before returning to the original position. He should repeat as before, but bring his left elbow across to touch his right knee. The player should repeat in rhythm counting one each time his touch his elbow touches the opposite knee.

Develops: Abdominal and hip muscles.

Station 3: Astride jump

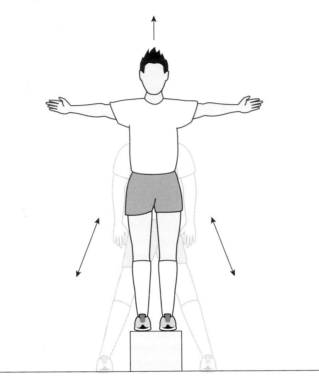

The player starts by standing astride a box. He then jumps upwards, bringing both feet together so that he is standing up straight on top of the box before jumping down to stand astride in the original position. Repeat rhythmically and count one each time you stand on top of the box.

Develops: Leg muscles.

Station 4: Back raise

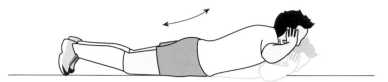

The player starts by lying on his front with legs outstretched behind him and hands at the side of his head. He then raises his body off the floor before lowering back to the original position. He should repeat this movement in a safe, rhythmical fashion and count one each time he comes to the end position and raises his body from the floor. Encourage the player to support his feet as he performs the exercise.

Develops: Back and stomach muscles.

Station 5: Press-up

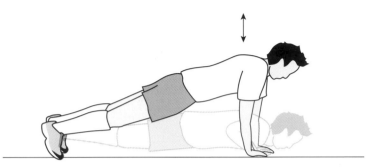

Get the player to start in the frontal support position with arms shoulder-width apart and bent, and body and legs flat on the floor. He then presses his arms into the floor until they are straight and his body is fully raised, and then he must return to the original position. Ask them to repeat in a rhythmical way ensuring that they keep their bodies straight throughout and count one each time they lock their arms into the straight position.

Develops: Arm and shoulder muscles.

Station 6: Step-up

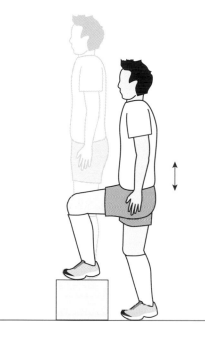

The player should start by standing directly in front of a box. He then steps on and off the box in a rhythmic four-count movement – left-right-left-right. They should then repeat, making sure that they keep their body and legs straight each time they stand on the box. To help them keep time, they can count one each time they stand on top of the box.

Develops: Leg muscles.

Station 7: Leg overs

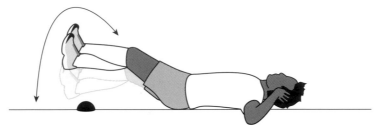

The player must start by lying on his back with his feet crossed and together. His legs should be held straight and his hands should be placed at the sides of his head. A small soft object is placed to one side of his feet. He must then raise his legs and twist his body a little, pushing them over the object to gently make contact with the floor on the far side before returning to the original central position. He should repeat in a rhythmical fashion on the other side and count one each time he touches the floor with his feet.

Develops: Stomach, hip, back and leg muscles.

Station 8: Squat jump

Start by bending your knees into the half-squat position with your body straight and arms held at the sides of your head. Thrust your legs upwards so that they straighten up and drive your body into an explosive jump. Land lightly in the original position and repeat the movement in a continuous rhythmical way, counting one each time you jump.

Develops: Leg muscles.

Station 9: Back press

The player should start by sitting outstretched in front of a low box with both arms bent, hands supporting his body on top of the box behind him. He then straightens his arms by pressing into the box to fully raise his body up before returning to the original position. Keeping his body and legs straight, he should repeat in a careful, rhythmical fashion. Get them to count one each time they fully straighten their arms.

Develops: Arm and shoulder muscles.

Station 10: Skipping

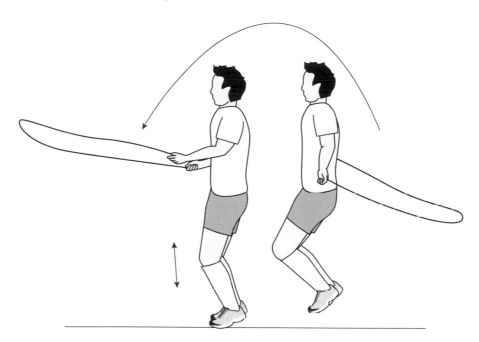

The player starts by holding the rope in his hands and skips in a two-footed fashion in a continuous rhythmical way, looking to land lightly each time. He should count one each time he skips over the circling rope.

Develops: Aerobic endurance and leg muscles.

SKILLS CIRCUIT

Purpose

To develop specific power, muscular and all-round endurance and agility.

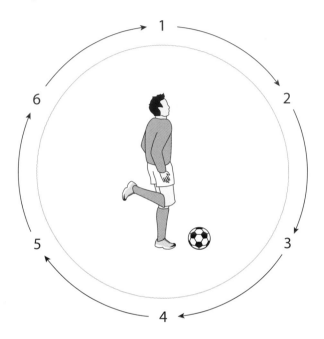

Organisation

As before, exercises are set up around an indoor or outdoor circuit. The players perform them either as a set number or within a set time. The totals can be recorded for each player, or even for the team, with a view to players looking to better their score each time. Here is a simple skills circuit that can be used by a coach looking to improve various components of fitness.

Station 1: Jump heading

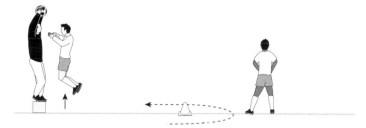

Players are in pairs, with one partner standing on a low box holding a football above his head whilst the other player stands at a cone some 10 yards away facing player one. The player at the cone runs to jump and head the ball, which is held in the hands of the partner, and then turns to run back around the cone and repeats the movement continuously. They should count one for each header and then change roles.

Station 2: Dribble and pass

One partner should proceed to dribble the ball around a slalom of poles before returning to pass the ball to his partner at the other end. The other player immediately returns the pass and the first player continues dribbling, counting one for each dribble completed. Partners then change roles.

Station 3: Throw-in

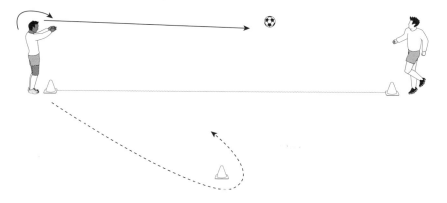

One player executes a correct throw-in for his partner to catch. He then runs around a cone set up approximately 10 yards away and returns to receive a pass from his partner, where he can pick the ball up from the floor and repeat the throw-in. Players should count each throw-in made and then change roles.

Station 4: Slide tackle

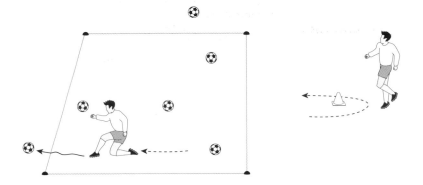

One player stands at a cone approximately 10 yards or so from a 10-yard square with six footballs spread around inside this area. He proceeds to run from the cone into the square and performs a correct and safe slide tackle to push one ball out of the area. He then recovers quickly before running around the cone and repeating the skill. Record the time it takes to push the six footballs out of the square – the partner should try to beat this when they change roles.

Station 5: Shooting

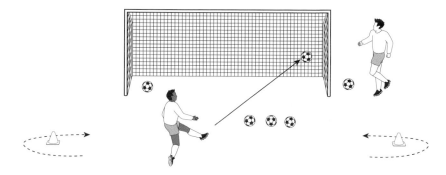

One player stands about 6 yards directly in front of a goal with a net and with a football at his feet. Two cones are placed at the sides of the ball about 20 yards apart. The player starts by running around the left cone and back to hit the ball hard with his left foot into the net. He then runs around the right cone and returns to strike the ball with his right foot into the net. He runs around alternate cones and hits the ball with alternate feet continuously whilst his partner quickly replaces the ball in the central position from the net each time. The partners change roles and compete against each other to see who can score most goals in the given time.

Station 6: Dribble-turn-pass

A player collects the football from behind the set line and dribbles it forwards towards a wall or rebound surface. He plays the ball off the surface and controls it whilst turning with it and dribbles it back to his partner, passing the ball to him. His partner returns the shot pass to him and he repeats the skill. Count the number of turns he achieves in the given time and encourage his partner to try to beat his score.

CONDITIONED GAMES

Purpose

Small or larger football games can be adapted or conditioned in various ways to intensify the training load on players. The advantage of this is that the movements and fitness components that the players develop will be more realistic and have greater transfer to the actual game itself and should improve their fitness in a more specific way. The following games will improve most components of football fitness:

Follow your pass

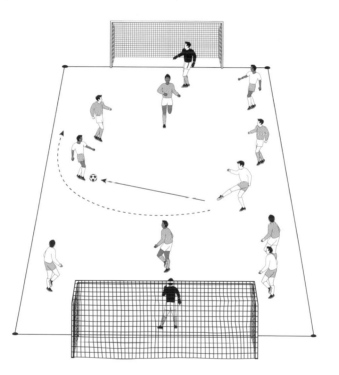

Play a small game with the condition that each player must follow their pass. Failure to do this means that the team forfeits possession of the ball, which goes to the other team. To ensure each player runs that little bit further ask him to perform an overlap run where he must run on the outside, past the player that he has passed the ball to. This will ensure plenty of movement and running within the actual game.

One v one

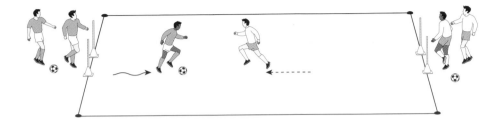

Various games of one v one can be organised by a creative coach. These games can be very strenuous and physically demanding for players and need to be organised and handled carefully by the coach. Design them so that players play for small, intensive bursts of time before allowing them small 'recovery' periods. This small game has two teams numbered from one to three who stand behind their respective small goals. The coach calls a number, say number two, whereupon the number twos from both teams emerge and play one v one against each other. The coach can control the intensity and length of time of each game and the entire training sequence.

Man-to-man marking

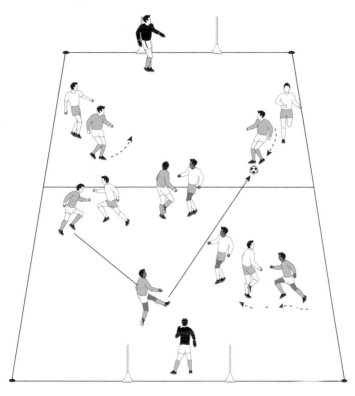

The coach can organise games where players are matched together in a one v one situation. One effective game is to play 'man-marking', where different pairs of players alternately have to 'mark' or try to evade their partner, marking them out of the game. This is very hard work, but used properly by the coach for the appropriate length of time it can be very effective in developing players' aerobic, anaerobic and speed-endurance fitness.

Summary

Many games and game-like activities can be adapted to emphasise the fitness elements for individuals, groups or the team as a whole. The coach can use conditions, or overload one team by giving them an extra player(s) so that the other team need to work harder. He can also change the dimensions or size of the playing area so that the players have longer distances to run. Remember, games can be used in conjunction with the more formal methods such as weight training, etc., to provide a more comprehensive training programme for your players, and team whilst keeping them more happy at the same time!

Goalkeepers need to be mentally tough as well as having the physical, technical and tactical attributes to enable them to play in this position. Ben Foster, the Manchester United and England custodian, has had to withstand criticism for some of his displays. However, like any top-class goalkeeper, he has put in extra work on the training ground to eliminate any potential faults and has placed himself back in contention for the number one spot for club and country. This is a good lesson for any aspiring young goalkeeper wanting to reach the top.

Index

Notes

Also available

Youth Football Coaching: Developing your team throughout the season by Simon Jay

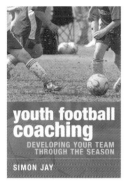

Youth Football Coaching is essential reading for all those who coach 11-a-side to 11–18 year olds, and want to plan and deliver structured, professional training sessions to assist their team to reach full potential throughout the season. Also valuable for those studying for Level 2 or Level 3 (UEFA B) coaching qualifications, this book is the crucial step to developing a foolproof coaching strategy.

101 Youth Football Drills: Age 7–11 (3rd edn)
101 Youth Football Drills: Age 12–16 (3rd edn)
by Malcolm Cook

Designed specifically for players within the specified age-range, these manuals contain a wide range of progressive practice drills to help young players develop. Fun, educational and challenging, all drills are illustrated and cover the essential technical skills including: warming up, dribbling and running with the ball, passing, shooting, heading, crossing, goalkeeping and warming down.

Football – Raise Your Mental Game by Richard Nugent and Steve Brown

Football – Raise Your Mental Game takes principles from a number of areas of psychology and applies them to football in an easy-to-read, accessible way. Includes chapters on self-confidence, keeping focussed and performing consistently, getting motivated for matches, managing anger, relaxation and dealing with nerves, and positive mental practice.

Also available

Soccer Coaching: The professional way **by Malcolm Cook**

Soccer Coaching: The Professional Way includes all the information and guidance that soccer coaches need to develop the skills required to manage a football team successfully. Each chapter addresses an aspect of coaching, from how to plan a coaching process to communicating effectively with players and developing a scouting programme to identify new talent. Other topics covered include:

- developing a coaching style and planning a coaching programme
- coaching methods and team coaching
- motivating the team
- coaching for performance.

Available from all good bookshops or online. For more details on these and other A&C Black sport and fitness titles, please go to www.acblack.com.